Twayne's Theatrical Arts Series

Warren French
EDITOR

Francis Ford Coppola

Francis Ford Coppola

Francis Ford Coppola

ROBERT K. JOHNSON

Suffolk University

BOSTON

Twayne Publishers

1977

Published by Twayne Publishers
A Division of G. K. Hall & Co.
Copyright © 1977 by G. K. Hall & Co.
All Rights Reserved
First Printing

Library of Congress Cataloging in Publication Data

Johnson, Robert K
  Francis Ford Coppola.

  (Twayne's theatrical arts series)
  Bibliography: p. 187–90.
  Includes index.
  1. Coppola, Francis Ford, 1939–
PN1998.A3C7855   791.43'0233'0924   77-6357
ISBN 0–8057–9252–X

MANUFACTURED IN THE UNITED STATES OF AMERICA

Contents

About the Author

ROBERT KENNETH JOHNSON was born in New York City. He attended Queens College, New York University, and Hofstra College, receiving his B.A. in English from Hofstra. Aided by a Woodrow Wilson Fellowship, he was able to obtain an M.A. degree at Cornell University in 1960. Denver University's English Department awarded him a Fellowship; and he concluded his Ph. D. work there in 1963.

He has taught at several schools, including Loretto Heights College, DePauw University, and the University of Missouri at Kansas City. Since 1968 he has taught in Boston at Suffolk University, where he is a Professor of English. In addition to courses in Modern American Poetry and Great Books of World Literature, he offers two film courses, The World on Film and Talking Pictures.

Interested in writing as well as in teaching, during the years he has had various kinds of original work published. Professor Johnson's publications include movie reviews, book reviews, literary criticism, short stories, essays, and poetry. Some of his articles have focused on Robert Lowell, William Carlos Williams, and Wallace Stevens. A critical essay on Richard Wilbur, written for *The Fifties*, was later quoted in *Contemporary Literary Criticism*. Approximately one hundred of his poems have appeared in various magazines and a book-length collection of his poetry, *Blossoms Of The Apricot*, was published in 1975. An expanded second edition will be published in the near future.

Editor's Foreword

ANDREW SARRIS in *The American Cinema* describes Francis Ford Coppola as "probably the first reasonably talented and sensibly adaptable directorial talent to emerge from a university curriculum in film-making." When this judgment was made ten years ago, Coppola had directed only four relatively modest feature pictures; *The Godfather* saga lay in the unguessed future. That two-part project and the lavish reception it has received at both the box office and the Academy Awards programs have made Coppola one of the most conspicuous figures in today's film world. As a result college film programs are now watched with new interest.

Yet the glamorous reputation gained from *The Godfathers* is not Coppola's only distinction. In a business controlled by vast conglomerates, in which millions of dollars are gambled on each production, Coppola has brashly insisted upon making an unprofitable but artistically unique series of "personal" films—*You're a Big Boy Now*, *The Rain People*, and *The Conversation*. He has already made several fortunes and dissipated them on such "personal" projects and in efforts to help other young filmmakers. As this book goes to press, Coppola is bogged down in one of his most grandiose projects, a film with the working title *Apocalypse Now*, upon which millions of dollars have been spent with no end yet in sight. How will it come out? Coppola creates cliff-hangers off screen as well as on.

Whatever the fate of this project, it is surely time—though Coppola is still under forty—for a study of what he has accomplished so far and how he has been able to do it.

As Bob Johnson points out in this book, Coppola has not yet—despite successes and honors—produced a thoroughly satisfying film. In some ways, his first major effort, *You're a Big Boy Now*, remains his best—the most spontaneous, the best designed. I remember how it enchanted me when I first saw it and roused my continuing interest in this "college kid" director. Unfortunately, it was not a popular success, because, I suspect—like Theodore Flicker's *The President's Analyst* (my great "lost" favorite)—it was too flippantly tough-minded for the self-consciously serious young iconoclasts of the late 1960s, who preferred the sentimental self-indulgences of *The Graduate* and *Easy Rider*. Coppola's pictures have never been one-sided; he sees the follies of young rebels as well as the Establishment's. Thus to appreciate his films requires a capacity for objectivity and an ironic view of one's self that viewers rarely bring to the theater.

If *You're a Big Boy Now* had been a greater success, Coppola might subsequently have had less trouble about the commodity he most complains of lacking—time. Because he is a charming sales-man from all accounts, his problem has not been so much to get money as to work out his projects before the camera starts rolling.

The principal thing that I have learned from Johnson's perceptive account is that, trying to emulate predecessors like D. W. Griffith and Orson Welles—who have spectacularly turned "one-man shows" into their greatest films—Coppola has probably tended to try to do too much by himself without contemplatively assessing his strengths and weaknesses. Johnson repeatedly stresses that Coppola's principal problems have been with pacing and plotting. In the light of this, it strikes me that the most astute analysis of Coppola as artist is Gary Arnold's concerning the director's collaboration with Mario Puzo on *The Godfather:* "Coppola's exquisite sensibility refines the crudities out of Puzo's story, while that brutal, archetypal, melodramatic story concentrates and intensifies Coppola's abilities . . ." (see Chapter 7).

What Coppola brings to the screen—like Fellini and Antonioni, whom he apparently much admires—is a rare sensibility, a perception of the subtle effects of experience upon people. Like the novelist Joseph Conrad, he seeks not to bring us messages, but to make us "see." Only the future can reveal whether he can find the right kind of sympathetic collaborators to provide the strong dramatic materials that he can illuminate with his sensitive insight into what "looks right," so that audiences may be provided with the cathartic but essentially visual experience the cinema should provide.

If Coppola succeeds, his work so far and this book will indeed be

Editor's Forward

only a beginning. While we wait, however, certainly the man who created "The Godfather" pictures commands our attention for what he has so far accomplished.

WARREN FRENCH

Preface

I UNDERTOOK to write this book because I think Francis Ford Coppola's career is a very interesting one and deserves to be described in detail. He has become the prototype of the young man who, while still in school, decides to study to become a Hollywood director or writer. Also I like some of Coppola's films very much, and I wrote the book in order to discuss those films at length.

The biographical material about someone who becomes famous early in life has a way of becoming polished ever more smoothly as time goes on. For this reason, it is worthwhile to synthesize the earliest accounts before they are completely superseded by tidier renditions. Because Coppola is so articulate, I have included many of his comments. In fact, whenever possible I have deliberately refrained from paraphrasing (a most common device of those writing biographies of Hollywood personalities). All the chapter titles are drawn from Coppola's remarks. I have also quoted a fair amount of material depicting what occurred during the making of Coppola's films, for this material offers a realistic account of the workaday film world.

My desire to comment on some of Coppola's films made my commenting on all of his films obligatory. Some of them are failures; and I have explained why I think this is the case. I have also cited the shortcomings in those films I consider, on the whole, highly commendable. However, my primary critical motivation was—and remained—a positive one. *You're A Big Boy Now* delighted me the first time I saw it (and on all subsequent occasions). And I want everyone to see it. I want everyone to see Coppola's other films too, for I think his talent is such that all of his films—good, middling, and poor—deserve special attention.

But, truth to tell, another major reason I wrote this book is that I love to talk about movies—because I love movies. My sister and I have always loved movies. Children of the Depression, we, and often the rest of our family as well, were nevertheless able to go to all the low-priced movie houses within walking distance of our 2363 Valentine Avenue apartment in the Bronx. (June Allyson lived in the apartment house next to ours. She was literally The Girl Next Door.) My sister and I would see and relish double or triple features, plus all the extras such as "The Eyes And Ears Of The World." To this day, I tingle with excitement every time I watch the "Previews of Coming Attractions."

ROBERT K. JOHNSON

Acknowledgments

I AM HAPPY to have the chance to express my gratitude to those who helped me with this book. I want to thank Dean Michael Ronayne, Dr. Stanley Vogel, and the other people at Suffolk University who were responsible for my obtaining a sabbatical leave so that I could concentrate on my manuscript. I did the majority of my research at the Needham Library; and my thanks go to Mrs. Vivian D. McIver and her staff for all their assistance. I also appreciate the aid given to me at Hofstra University by Miss Stroh, Mrs. Reagan, and Mrs. Miller. Dr. Bernard Beckerman, now Dean of the School of the Arts at Columbia University, deserves a special thanks for taking the time to respond to my letter of inquiry. And I particularly want to thank Warren French for his guidance, suggestions, and encouragement. Finally, my special thanks to my wife Pat not only for scrutinizing my manuscript, but for assuming so many of my domestic responsibilities in order that I might work without interruption.

Thanks are due to The Museum of Modern Art/Film Stills Archive, the Academy of Motion Picture Arts and Sciences, Paramount Pictures, and Warner Brothers - Seven Arts, Inc. for film stills used in this volume.

*   *   *

To Jeanette

Chronology

1939   Born on April 7 in Detroit, Michigan, Francis Ford Coppola
        is the second of three offspring. His parents are Carmine, a
        symphony orchestra flutist, and Italia Coppola.

1957–   Attends Hofstra College on a drama scholarship; directs sev-
1960   eral plays, including *Inertia* (an original musical comedy for
        which he also wrote the lyrics), *A Streetcar Named Desire*,
        and *A Delicate Touch* (an original musical comedy for which
        he wrote both the lyrics and the book), edits and contributes
        to the student magazine, *The Word*. Earns his B.A. degree
        in 1960 and enters the University of California, Los Angeles,
        film school, where he studies on campus for two years.

1962   Hired by Roger Corman and works on *The Tower of London*
        (1962), *Battle Beyond the Sun* (1963), *The Young Racers*
        (1963), and *The Terror* (1964).

1963   *Dementia 13*, written and directed by Coppola, is released.
        The set director is Eleanor Neil, whom Coppola marries
        right after completing the film. They eventually have three
        children, Gian-Carlo, Roman, and Sophia.

1966   Hired earlier by Seven Arts as a scriptwriter, Coppola is
        given partial screen credit for two films released in 1966 to
        generally unfavorable reviews, *This Property Is Condemned*
        and *Is Paris Burning?*

1967   *You're A Big Boy Now*, directed and adapted for the screen
        by Coppola, shown nationally, brings his first laudatory re-
        views; enables him to earn his Master of Arts degree at
        U.C.L.A.

1968   *Finian's Rainbow*, directed by Coppola, is severely criticized
        by the majority of critics.

1969   Written and directed by Coppola, *The Rain People* receives
        many negative comments, but wins (1970) an award at

Spain's San Sebastian International Cinema Festival. He is now in charge of American Zoetrope, a multimedia enterprise.

1970   Wins a 1970 Academy Award as co-author of the film-script for *Patton*.

1972   Wins 1972 Academy Award as co-author of the film-script for *The Godfather;* directs *The Godfather*, which is voted best picture of that year. Also directs Noel Coward's *Private Lives* for the American Conservatory Theatre in San Francisco and the American premiere of Gottfried von Einem's *The Visit of the Old Lady* for the San Francisco Opera Company. With Peter Bogdanovich and William Friedkin, he forms the Directors Company.

1973   Is executive producer of *American Graffiti*, directed by his friend George Lucas.

1974   Written and directed by Coppola, *The Conversation* is both praised and panned. It wins the highest award at Cannes Film Festival. *The Great Gatsby*, for which Coppola wrote the screen adaptation, receives mainly negative criticism. But *The Godfather, Part II* opens to high acclaim and is voted 1974 Academy Award for best picture; other Oscars come to Coppola as director and co-author of the film.

1975–   Becomes increasingly involved with filming *Apocalypse*
1976   *Now*, which he directs and rewrites from a script first done by John Milius.

1

"A Fantasy World"

Early Years

THE WAY Francis Ford Coppola entered the motion picture business was quite unusual—at least in comparison with the way many older film directors started their careers.

In *Each Man in His Time,* Raoul Walsh tells us that he, the son of a highly successful New York business man, was a sailor, an expert rope-twirler, a ranchhand in Texas, a gravedigger in Montana, and a "topper" (a rider who tamed fractious horses). Only at this point in his life did he, by chance, move even an inch of the way toward becoming a film director. While recuperating from a knee injury, he was hired to "ride" a horse on a treadmill in a theater production of *The Clansman.* Encouraged by a fellow actor, Walsh traveled to New York, signed a three-picture contract with Pathé Brothers, and then, switching to the now-legendary Biograph production unit, acted in movies with Blanche Sweet and the Gish sisters. Introduced to D. W. Griffith, he played the role of John Wilkes Booth in *The Birth of a Nation* and assisted in the directing of the battle scenes. Gradually given more power, Walsh directed such films as the original *The Thief of Bagdad, What Price Glory?, High Sierra,* and *White Heat.*

Chance, not determination, also played a pivotal role in the career of Frank Capra. As we learn from his autobiography *The Name Above the Title,* Capra, born of peasant stock in Sicily, came to the United States and made his way, despite family opposition, through grammar school, high school, and even college. After a stint in the Army and as a tutor, he spent three years travelling hobo-fashion in Arizona, Nevada, and California. In San Francisco, he—on a sudden impulse—hopped on a cable car. The conductor happened to show him an advertisement in the newspaper:

19

"Fireside Productions has announced it is revamping the old Jewish Gymnasium at Golden Gate Park into a Movie Studio." Capra went to the Gymnasium, fast-talked his way into being paid to make a film titled *Ballad of Fultah Fisher's Boarding House,* and became addicted to movie-making.

Coppola introduced a whole new pattern for film directors' biographies. For he wanted to be a filmmaker even when he was still quite young.

Coppola was born in Detroit, Michigan on April 7, 1939, the second of three children. The oldest was his brother, August, and the youngest was Talia, the baby of the family. Coppola's father, Carmine Coppola, was neither a Sicilian peasant nor a rich New Yorker. Of Neapolitan descent, Mr. Coppola was a concert flutist who played in several orchestras, including Toscanini's famous NBC Symphony orchestra. He also worked intermittently as a musical arranger for the stage shows presented at Radio City Music Hall.

But he wanted more. He wanted to be a successful and famous composer (an ambition that, ironically, he would only realize—in a way—through his son's films). Thwarted year after year, he became increasingly frustrated and bitter. The Coppola family moved again and again back and forth across the country. Later, Coppola spoke of this side of his early life quite candidly. "My childhood was very warm, very tempestuous, full of controversy and a lot of passion and shouting. My father, who is an enormously talented man, was the focus of all our lives . . . . Our lives centered on what we all felt was the tragedy of his career." Coppola related this curious anecdote. "I worked for Western Union one summer when I was 14 and, for some unknown reason—I still don't know *why*—I wrote a phony telegram to my father telling him he'd landed a job writing the musical score for such and such a film. I signed it with the name of the guy who was in charge of music at Paramount Pictures. My father was overjoyed and yelled, 'It's my break! It's my break!' And I had to tell him it wasn't true. He was heartbroken. Is that a terrible story?"[1]

Perhaps because the crises came so rapidly, to be in a state of anxiety became habitual with Coppola. When an adult, he seemed at times almost to court cliff-hanger dilemmas. He once remarked, "My wife tells me I put myself in these tight spots to justify my anxiety."[2]

In any case, despite the warmth and closeness of the Coppola family, there were other problems for the second son. For one thing, Coppola's brother August was far more socially popular than he was. In the eyes of his kid brother, August was clearly handsomer and smarter.[3] Coppola described himself at this time as "funny-looking, not good at school, near-sighted."[4]

Another important feature of his early life was, of course, the family's participation in the arts. His mother's father, Francesco Pennino, was also a skilled musician. His mother Italia at one time acted in films. August wrote and later became a professor of comparative literature. His sister, Talia, billed as Talia Shire, would appear in the two *Godfather* films and gain even more acclaim in *Rocky*.

All of these features of family life began to coalesce to produce another artist when Coppola was nine years old. It was at this time that he contracted polio, an illness that caused his legs to be always too short for the rest of his body. Confined to bed for a year, he played with puppets and created puppet theaters, watched television hour after hour, and read. "I got immersed in a fantasy world," he later remarked. "The popular kid is out having a good time. He doesn't sit around thinking about who he is or how he feels. But the kid who is ugly, sick, miserable or schlumpy sits around heartbroken and thinks."[5]

In 1949, because his father had a tape recorder and an 8-millimeter motion picture projector, Coppola began making films. "I used to have synchronized movies. Most of them I cut together from home movies my family had shot. I'd make myself the hero. I made money out of them, too. I'd show them to other kids in the neighborhood."[6]

By the time Coppola was in high school, he was seriously interested in theater, films, writing, and music. After having been enrolled in many schools because of his father's travels, he attended Cornwall-on-Hudson, a private school in upstate New York, as a music scholarship student. But he became angry when the book and lyrics he had written for a class musical were greatly altered. For this reason, he changed schools in his senior year and graduated from Great Neck High School on Long Island. When Coppola wrote the screenplay for *The Great Gatsby*, he knew his setting firsthand; Great Neck and Little Neck served as the model for Big Egg and Little Egg, the major setting in Scott Fitzgerald's novel.

It was just about this time that Coppola discovered the films of

Sergei Eisenstein. As he later recalled, "When I was about eighteen, I became very interested in Eisenstein. I became a disciple. I read all of his work and went to see his films at the Museum of Modern Art. And I was really dying to make a film. Taking my example from him, I went to theater school, and worked very hard. I directed lots of plays and I studied theater and I could light a set, build a set. I wanted to be very well rounded, very complete, to have that kind of background, because Eisenstein had started like that."[7]

In the fall of 1956, still not eighteen years old, Coppola entered Hofstra College (now Hofstra University). Interested in both writing and directing, he was awarded a drama scholarship by Dr. Bernard Beckerman, the head of the Drama Department. At this time Hofstra was small enough to allow an ambitious student the opportunity to make his way into several organizations and to become influential in all of them. Yet the school was big enough to supply such a student with plenty of classmates to help him complete any large-scale projects he had in mind.

While still a freshman, Coppola became the Music-Drama Editor of *The Word*, the student literary magazine. During that year he—for the first of many times—created quite a stir on campus among the students interested in the arts. The source of this excitement was a short story he wrote for *The Word*. The story was titled "Candide—or Pessimism," and the author's name was given as François-Marie Arouet de Coppola. The hero, Candide, lives in Great Neck and is tutored by a Dr. Grimes who assures him that he lives in the "worst of all previous worlds." At first Candide accepts his tutor's viewpoint and spurns the sexual advances made to him by his step-sister Cunegonde. However, after running away and having to "endure" gaining fame and fortune, and then running away again, Candide, near starvation and death in Jackson Heights, is nursed back to health by a "goddess" of beauty who turns out to be Cunegonde, remodeled by plastic surgery. When Dr. Grimes turns up to remind his pupil that the world is rotten, "Candide expelled Dr. Grimes from his life by kicking him in the backside frequently and hard." Leading Cunegonde back to bed, he says, " 'What kind of crap did they teach me when I was young.' "[8]

Coppola's fellow students were much impressed by two features of this freshman's story. In form, it was well-phrased and quick-moving—holding the reader's attention from beginning to end. The anti-intellectualism and anti-authoritarianism expounded in the content were even more appealing.

For anyone curious about Coppola's film career, this story is of interest for still other reasons. Cunegonde clearly foreshadows the aggressive female found especially in Coppola's "personal" films, as they have come to be described. Natalie, the heroine in *The Rain People*, takes the initiative concerning her own life. In *The Conversation*, Harry Caul decides not to see his female companion any more because she asks him too many questions. And in Coppola's first major film, *You're A Big Boy Now*, Barbara Darling, the young woman whom the naive Bernard worships, and all of the other females in the film are nothing if not aggressive.

The short story's fast-paced, episodic structure points to the film style used in *You're A Big Boy Now*. This would suggest, as Coppola claimed, that the film was not quite as influenced by the fast-paced, episodic Richard Lester-Beatles movies as film critics have insisted it is. Finally, the story's presentation of Candide's mounting rebelliousness and final rejection of the passive role unquestionably points toward *You're A Big Boy Now*. It also foreshadows the ever-intenser—if ultimately inept and fruitless—rebellion of Harry Caul in *The Conversation*.

In his first year and a half at Hofstra, Coppola wrote three other stories for *The Word*. His first published story was "The Garden of the Little Pink Princess." This story, too, anticipates Bernard's relationship with Barbara in *You're A Big Boy Now*. A young boy worships a still younger pink-princess of a girl—until he becomes disillusioned in her when he discovers that she, for a price, lets the neighborhood boys "look at her." Set in the Middle Ages, a third story, "The Battle of the Lions," is also not without interest. The most vivid writing focuses on machinery. Coppola devotes almost one whole page of this four-page story to descriptions of various typical medieval siege-weaponry, while the plot's climax occurs when two armies unveil the newest weapon known to the Western world at that time—the cannon. Coppola's preoccupation with technology, with mechanical gadgets of all kinds, long predates *The Conversation*.

The Fall 1957 issue of *The Word* contained "Del Vecchio," the last story Coppola wrote for the magazine. It is also his weakest story. It centers on a man who prayed to God to make him "a neuter sex," and later realizes that his wish has been granted. Too pat, and more than a bit muddled as to just what point the author is trying to make, the story nonetheless reminds us that many of the men in the films for which Coppola wrote original screenplays are not dominating *macho* figures. Related to this, Coppola once commented, "I'm convinced that men and women are basically very similar in many more respects than we've been brought up to believe. We've been taught so-called masculine roles, just as women have been programed into so-called feminine ones. But the lines aren't so clearly drawn anymore, partly because of the women's movement." Then he added, "I know a great many heterosexual women who are very masculine in many ways, and many heterosexual men who are very feminine. I include myself among the latter and I always have."[9]

Coppola remained Music-Drama Editor of *The Word* through the Winter 1959 issue. But well before this time he was devoting his primary energies elsewhere.

From the time he was a freshman, he was directly involved in Hofstra's theater productions. It was a fine time for a student to be interested in theater; for during the years Coppola attended Hofstra, a number of especially talented students were active in drama. One of Coppola's fellow drama majors was Joel Oliansky, who later won Emmy-award recognition for his scripts for *The Senator* and *The Law*. Many other students became professional performers, including the singer Lainie Kazan, Lorraine Serabian, Ellen Weston, and Ron Colby (who worked on some of Coppola's first film efforts). James Caan, who later starred in *The Rain People* and *The Godfather*, attended Hofstra for a short time and worked backstage with Coppola on the school's 1958 production of *Hamlet*.

As he had hoped to do, Coppola worked on many different facets of theater. As a freshman he had minor acting roles in *Once in a Lifetime*, *Best Foot Forward*, and *As You Like It*. In the last-mentioned production he was also a member of the stage crew. The following year he was even more active. He was on the lighting crew for *Hamlet*, and head of the *Blood Wedding* lighting crew. He was construction crew chief for *Light Up The Sky* and *Of Thee I Sing*. In this Gershwin musical he appeared on stage for the last time at Hofstra. More significantly, he was partially responsible for the show's updated dialogue and lyrics. In 1959, he was a member of the *Picnic* stage crew.

Long before the *Picnic* production, however, Coppola had created much more of a stir as a director than he had as the author of

"Candide" and other stories. Very early in his stay at Hofstra he directed a presentation of Eugene O'Neill's "The Rope" that won him the Dan H. Lawrence Award for outstanding direction. Dr. Beckerman, in fact, considered it the best student-directed show he had ever seen. As a result of the high quality of Coppola's workmanship Dr. Beckerman gave Coppola quite a free rein.

Coppola used his freedom, and his growing campus power, most productively. He produced *Inertia*, the first play at Hofstra ever to be entirely written, produced, and directed by students. Joel Oliansky did the book, based on the H. G. Wells story "The Man Who Could Work Miracles." Steve Lawrence composed the music. But Coppola was primarily responsible for the outstanding quality of the final presentation. He conceived the idea for the show, wrote the lyrics for the music, and, with marked skill, directed the production.

It was the solid success of *Inertia* that led many people on campus to believe firmly and remain convinced that Coppola possessed serious first-rate talent. During his first two years at Hofstra, Coppola's work never gained him *sustained* esteem among the majority of his fellow students. For in those years Coppola never "came on strong" as a personality. Conversation did not stop when he entered the student cafeteria or a room at a party. If heads turned in his direction, they soon turned away again. Soft-spoken, he did not automatically take command of a conversation he joined. Often he just sat, saying little—and none of that very memorable. Consequently, until *Inertia*, many of Coppola's fellow students were always a little surprised by the success of each of his endeavors.

Coppola became "a big man on campus" not because he exuded an overwhelming charisma. He became well known and respected strictly as a result of his steady series of achievements. Before the success of *Inertia*, he had to work hard to convince others to accept his ideas (in Hollywood, he would be praised and admired as a salesman). After *Inertia*, he gained his way at Hofstra much more easily.

Coppola later described this time in his life. "Hofstra was very influential in my life. I went from being an average student to being at the center of college theater. It was the first time I had the real responsibility of running my own show. I was relatively as powerful there as I am now in the larger world."[10]

In his senior year Coppola directed a much-admired production of *A Streetcar Named Desire*. He also wrote the book and lyrics for, and produced, *A Delicate Touch*, another musical comedy, with a plot suggested by a scene in the film *Heartbeat*.

Yet it would be wrong to say that Coppola had wandered completely away from his early interest in filmmaking.

While still at Hofstra, Coppola founded a Cinema Workship. In his junior year he sold his car in order to buy a 16-millimeter camera and make a movie. He devised the story himself; it featured a mother who spends the day in the country with her children. After she shows them the beautiful scenery, she falls asleep. When she wakes up, the children are gone. Commenting on the project, Coppola said, "The idea was that everything that had seemed so beautiful before now becomes ugly to her because it represents a possible danger to the missing children. I wanted to experiment with this kind of looking at the same thing two ways. I shot part of it but never finished it. I just didn't have the technical expertise."[11]

In hopes of gaining this expertise, Coppola entered the film school at the University of California at Los Angeles (UCLA) as a graduate student in 1960. All in all, it did not prove to be a happy experience for him. He later explained some of the reasons for this.

Despite his curiosity about technology, Coppola at Hofstra had deliberately sought more than a technological knowledge of filmmaking. In his view, most potential filmmakers in film schools "get so hung up—handling film is so much fun, so exciting—that they tend to bypass content and acting, the other things which eventually the film will make use of. They go into it with just technique,"[12] He found this to be true with regard to many students.

Another problem for Coppola at UCLA was his youth. He was younger—in some cases, much younger—than the majority of his fellow students. Idealistic, he had hoped to find the kind of *La Bohème* camaraderie among artists that he had daydreamed of while in high school. It was no small matter to him. When, after the success of the *Godfather* films, he was asked what made him happy, excluding his film work, he replied, "What brings me the greatest joy is the company of nice people and to be able to go through all the rituals with them, to eat dinner with them, cook with them, talk with them. I'm very European in that respect."[13]

He admitted afterwards that during his UCLA days he was too beguiled by his lingering daydreams. "My fantasy was you're working on the films and drinking wine at night, and there are beautiful

girls who are working on the films and you're all in it together."
What he discovered, however, was that "it wasn't like that. It was
very lonely."[14]

Other sources of Coppola's disenchantment with the film school's
environment were not solely the result of his immaturity. Coppola,
primarily a doer rather than a talker, felt that too many of his fellow
students were too much the opposite. Some of them "stood around
talking very impressively about how lousy Hollywood films were
and how *they* could really make great films."[15] But that was all they
did.

He was disappointed with the school administration, too. What
he wanted to know—and what many other students wanted to
know—was how to make a film. "Everyone in the school had that
same question in mind," he stated later. "For an answer we got
Stanley Kramer coming to lecture us on how successful he was."[16]

Disgruntled, he proceeded to do something that later allowed
people who disliked or were envious of him to snicker, and something that caused his friends and fans to feel embarrassed on his
behalf. He directed three "nudie" films.

Although tepidly tame by comparison with films presented later
in the 1960s and 1970s, when they were first shown nudie films
were thought by many people to be about as far out as movies could
go this side of stag films. In plot, they were little more than diluted
burlesque sketches. As far as their displays of the human body were
concerned, the films were milder than some present-day films put
in the Parental Guidance Category.

The first such film Coppola worked on was titled *The Peeper*. "It
was a cute little premise," he recalled, "about a little man who
discovers that they are shooting pin-ups near his house. The whole
film dealt with his attempts to see what was going on. Every method
he used would backfire. He would haul a gigantic telescope up to his
room—twelve feet long—and he would focus it but all he would see
would be bellybutton. Then he would do something else, and *that*
would backfire."

This film was purchased by "a company that had made a nudie
western about a cowboy who had been kicked in the head and saw
all the cows as naked ladies. It was terrible. They hired me to
combine my film with that film, and that was called *The Wide Open
Spaces*." Still another company hired him "for a few days to take a
dumb German black-and-white film and add five three-minute col-

or, 3-D nudie sketches to it. That was called *The Belt Girls and the Playboy*."[17]

Coppola never felt abashed about his work on these three films. "It was the only scene I could find that actually gave you a chance to fool around with a camera and cut a film."[18]

According to his own recollections, however, Coppola's work at UCLA did help him gain still more practical knowledge about filmmaking. One of his teachers was Dorothy Arzner. She had gained praise as a film editor on such films as *Blood and Sand* and *The Covered Wagon* and as the director of fifteen movies. Joan Crawford, Clara Bow, Frederic March, Rosalind Russell, and Katharine Hepburn were some of the stars cast in her productions. Coppola later singled her out as having been particularly helpful to him on both an artistic level and a personal level.[19]

Nevertheless, Coppola wanted more than he could find either at UCLA or by doing nudie films.

Roger Corman

A notice on the UCLA film school's bulletin board triggered Coppola's next move. The notice announced that Roger Corman was offering film work.

By the 1970s, a young person who worked for Corman was in a position many other young people greatly envied. But at the time Coppola decided to accept Corman's offer, his decision generated no envy.

Roger Corman's early biography resembles Frank Capra's more than it does Francis Ford Coppola's. Like Capra, Corman attended a California school in order to obtain a degree in engineering. Like Capra, he served in the armed forces and afterwards did not do much of anything for a few years. So, too, the turning point in Corman's life occurred by chance.

After having worked at various odd jobs, and collecting unemployment checks in between, Corman became a stagehand at a television station and then a reader for a literary agent. "While I was with the agent," Corman said later, "I saw all the crap that was coming in from guys who were writing scripts for B movies." Like many another, Corman thought he could write stories at least as good as those he was reading. Unlike many another, he was right. "I sat down and spent a lot of nights doing a script called 'Highway

Dragnet.' " Through his agent-employer, the script was sold to Allied Artists for $4,000.

With that money, plus money he borrowed from his family and friends, Corman wrote and produced another script. The story took place in the Yucatan; the filming took place at Malibu Beach. Corman had $12,000 to work with. The film, *Monster from the Ocean Floor*, was produced in six days—for $12,000. In its initial release, the movie grossed $100,000.[20]

Corman formed Roger Corman Productions. The success of his enterprises is now legendary. One of Corman's first featured actors was the then-unknown Jack Nicholson. Other newcomers employed by Corman included Ellen Burstyn, Robert DeNiro, Peter Fonda, Diane Ladd, Martin Scorsese, Haskell Wexler, and Robert Towne. In 1967, Corman bought several Russian films. Needing someone to cut them and shoot extra footage, he hired Peter Bogdanovich. During the first weeks Bogdanovich worked for him, Corman found himself in a bind. Threatened with a lawsuit by Boris Karloff, Corman had agreed to give Karloff $15,000 for only two days' work in a picture which would also include footage from an earlier picture Karloff made for Corman.

Corman called Bogdanovich into his office and announced that Bogdanovich was now going to have his chance to make a movie. He then detailed the "special" conditions under which Bogdanovich would have to work. Bogdanovich decided to have Karloff play a horror-film star who, early in the story, watches one of his own movies (the footage from Karloff's earlier picture). Bogdanovich added a psychopathic killer to the plot, a killer whom Karloff eventually prevents from committing mass murder.[21] The film, *Targets*, got excellent reviews, is still revived, and started Bogdanovich on a path that led to *The Last Picture Show* and other film successes.

Not long ago Coppola said, "There are a handful of directors today who have total authority and deserve it. And then there are a lot of other directors who really ought to be working with strong producers and strong writers, but they all think they're Stanley Kubrick." Then he stressed his point: "The *auteur* theory is fine, but to exercise it you have to qualify, and the only way you can qualify is by having *earned* the right to have control."[22]

Coppola continued to learn his trade—and, so, to move a little closer toward earning the right to control major film productions—by working for Corman. "Having gotten into the nudie racket," he summarized, "I started to move up the exploitation film ladder. I was willing to do anything to get to make more films, and the best opportunity was in the field of the exploitation film."

His UCLA student peers were not happy with him. "I was very seriously criticized by a lot of people my own age for my decision to go into exploitation films. I was a copout because I was willing to compromise." Once again, Coppola's reasoning was pragmatic. "No matter how you look at it, it costs a lot of money to make films. You don't make films on anything but money—and whatever talent you can bring to them."[23] Nor could you hone whatever talent you possessed unless you found work in your field.

While working on his first Roger Corman exploitation film, Coppola was himself exploited. He did the dubbing for *Battle Beyond the Sun* for $200–250, and worked at it for approximately six months. "Outrageous," Coppola later commented, "but I just wanted to get in that office because it sounded like they were really going to make movies there."[24]

Coppola was not at all hesitant about translating a Russian science fiction film into English. "I didn't understand a word of Russian but wasn't too worried about it since I figured that the original picture would have to be changed beyond recognition anyhow." He guessed correctly. "In one scene, for example, a Russian astronaut sees the figure of a Golden Astronaut—presumably a symbol of Hope—standing on a crag holding a golden flare. It was really lovely. Roger said, 'We've got to put two monsters up on that crag.' " The monsters were matted in through optical effects. "Roger wanted one monster to be a male sex symbol and the other to be a female sex symbol. Obviously, one had to devour the other." Coppola protested that this was going too far, but it was done all the same. The result was "sex and violence where the Russians had the Golden Astronaut of Hope."[25]

Battle Beyond the Sun gave Coppola his first screen credit.

Coppola worked as a dialogue director on Corman films. He also engaged in a bit of "acting." "I tried to impress Roger," he said later. "I'd deliberately work all night so when he'd arrive in the morning he'd see me slumped over the moviola. He started to see me as an all-purpose guy."[26]

One day, when Corman asked Coppola if he knew a sound man Corman could use for *The Young Racers*, Coppola told him that *he* was a sound man. "I got the job and immediately went home, got hold of the book on the Perfectone sound recorder, and started reading, 'Push button A . . .' So I went to Europe, recorded the racing footage for *The Young Racers*, and Roger was eventually happy with what I gave him."[27]

On still another occasion, Corman handed Coppola a problem similar to the one Corman later gave to Bogdanovich. Corman finished *The Raven*, but still had use of the sets. He informed Coppola that Boris Karloff had agreed to shoot two days' worth of film on the leftover sets. "My job," said Copola, "was to figure out what to do with the two days' worth of shooting, to try to make some kind of sense out of it all." In other words, the footage had been shot before there was a plot.

"For example, in one part of the film, a young soldier from Napoleon's army (Jack Nicholson played him) comes to this castle and meets Karloff." Karloff's character does not want the soldier in the castle. "So what does he do? He kills the soldier's horse. I've got to figure out why Karloff killed the horse when he wanted the soldier to leave!"[28]

This film was titled *The Terror*. Aided by Coppola (credited as Associate Producer) and by Jack Nicholson—who directed himself in one sequence—Corman did complete production work on the film in a hurry. So, too, it was footage from *The Terror* that, a few years later, Corman told Bogdanovich to use in *Targets*.

Because Coppola, somehow or another, always came through for Corman, because Coppola "knew his man," and because Coppola desperately wanted to make a film of his own, Corman helped him fulfill his desire to direct a picture. The decision came while Corman and Coppola were in Europe working on *The Young Racers*. Coppola knew that Corman would very much like to use the crew that he already had transported to Europe to make more than just one film. Quickly, Coppola created an idea for a picture that he would direct.

"I sold the picture to Roger on the basis of one scene. The time is late at night. The place is Dublin. A woman comes out of a castle. She is carrying a bag. She stops, opens the bag, and takes out five dolls. She ties strings around the necks of the dolls, then attaches the strings to a weight. Then the woman takes off all her clothes and dives into a pond. She places the weight on the bottom of the pond, and the dolls start to float up toward the surface. The woman starts to turn in the water, and there she finds the perfectly preserved body of a seven-year-old girl with her hair floating in the current. The woman rushes to the surface and screams the words: 'Axed to death!' Roger said, 'You've got a picture, kid.' "

Coppola added, "I had no idea what the woman was doing there."[29]

Corman put up $20,000. Coppola wrote a full-length script in three days. Corman sent a personal representative to Ireland where the film was to be shot. This woman was supposed to co-sign all the checks. But Coppola talked her into making over all the money to him immediately and then he put it in a special account under his own name.

This last move soon proved particularly important. For, in Ireland, Coppola talked with the English producer Raymond Stross, who said he had heard that Coppola was making a movie. Stross assumed that the filming was already under way. Coppola let the (false) assumption stand. Soon he had another $20,000 to work with, the money Stross gave him for the British rights to the film "in progress." "When Corman heard about this," Coppola reported, "he wanted to withdraw the initial production money, but I had put it in another account, remember."[30]

Dementia 13 (1963)

Coppola, spurred by Corman, knew exactly what effect he was after. "The film . . . was meant to be an exploitation film, a *Psycho*-type film."[31] Later he said, "I have seen more guys die . . . because they tried to straddle the art film and the exploitation film and finally ended up with neither. They would say, 'Okay, we're going to do *Freak Out*, but we're going to put some *relationships* in there,' and they would end up with something that wasn't good enough as an art film or funky enough as an exploitation film. When I was working on *Dementia 13*, I got telegrams from Roger Corman every other day asking for more sex and violence, more sex and violence."[32]

But making *Dementia 13* was not all "wheeling and dealing." It was also fun. Coppola invited his California friends to come over and become part of the action. Later he reminisced, "We were young and making a feature film!" He also said, "It was the only film I ever enjoyed working on."[33]

Among the group of Americans who traveled to Ireland in 1962 to take part in the production was Eleanor Neil. Her name appears in the credits as set director. After finishing *Dementia 13*, Coppola was scheduled to work on a film in Yugoslavia. Instead, he married Eleanor and came home to the United States.

When asked his opinion of the film in retrospect, Coppola replied, "I think it showed promise. It was imaginative. It wasn't totally cliché after cliché. Very beautiful visuals. In many ways, it had some of the nicest visuals I've ever done. Mainly, because I composed every shot. In the present circumstances, you never have the time. So you just leave it to others."[34]

The plot of *Dementia 13* first focuses on John Haloran and his wife Louise. While out rowing on a lake that is part of the Haloran estate in Ireland, the couple begin to argue because Louise will profit from Lady Haloran's will only as long as her husband, who has a bad heart, remains alive. Because of his mounting anger and the strain of rowing, John dies of a heart attack. Louise pushes his body into the lake and leads the rest of the family—Lady Haloran and her other two sons Richard and Billy—to believe that John has flown to New York.

Lady Haloran grieves morbidly for her long-dead daughter Kathleen, and Louise decides to drive her insane. But while in the lake pursuing this plan (the revised version of the origianl scene Coppola convincingly described to Corman), she is axed to death. Shortly before her death, Kane, Richard's fiancée, arrives. She vainly tries to talk Richard into leaving the estate; she also sympathizes with Billy, still subject to nightmares pertaining to Kathleen's death.

Events move rapidly to a climax. Simon, an old friend of the family, is also axed to death while hunting on the property. Lady Haloran is in Kathleen's old playhouse when it is smashed to pieces by the same ax-wielder. Justin Caleb, the family doctor, orders the lake drained and devises a scheme to flush out the murderer during the reception following the wedding of Richard and Kane. His plan is successful. It is revealed that Billy killed his sister Kathleen and is also responsible for the recent murders. He is shot and killed while attempting to murder Kane.

Nothing in this film would lead the viewer to predict that the person who wrote and directed it would later win an armful of Oscars. The acting is, at best, pedestrian. William Campbell

(Richard), Luana Anders (Louise), and Mary Mitchell (Kane) are
competent and no more. Others are not that good. Peter Read,
playing John Haloran, is often unconvincing. Patrick Magee, as
Doctor Caleb, overacts. Karl Schanzer, as Simon, is nothing less
than amateurish. Not one of the aristocrats appears in the least
aristocratic. Nor do the accents of some of the characters offer any
clue that they are supposed to be Irish.

Despite Coppola's insistence otherwise, the plot contains little
that is not a horror-movie cliché. It has the "haunted" castle with
many dark corridors and with sections "that have not been lived in
for years." There is a room kept just the way it was when its occu-
pant died. The background music is perfunctorily eerie. Almost all
of the action, of course, takes place at night. So, too, in order to
inject at least a little sex into the predominantly violent
proceedings, for no good reason Louise appears in her underwear in
one scene, and, in another, Kane appears in the sheerest of night-
ies.

There are also a few holes in the plot. The sudden and continued
absence of John and then Louise causes relatively little concern. It
is said that Louise might be "somewhere in town," and that is all.
The death of Simon and the destruction of the playhouse cause even
less comment. When the lake is drained, a headstone erected in
memory of Kathleen is discovered, but there is no sign of John's
corpse. Although Billy is a homicidal maniac, he gives no indication
of any psychological troubles except to admit he suffers from an
occasional nightmare.

Yet the film is not a bore. For while the acting is pedestrian, it
does not distract the audience's attention from the story. The plot,
though unoriginal, is still as diverting as most horror-film stories.
The clichés are present because they proved successful in previous
horror movies—and they prove successful in this one. In fact, the
plot implausibilities bother the viewer less than the plot implausibilities in *The Conversation* do. For, in good horror-film fashion, the pace in this early picture is fast enough to prevent the
viewer from having too much time to be very aware of implausibilities. Nor is the film technically embarrassing in any way.
Compared, for instance, with any of those Norman Mailer movies,
Dementia 13 stands out all the more clearly as a professional job.

Several features of the film can be singled out for praise. When the greedy Louise realizes that her husband has just died of a heart attack, she quite realistically does not shed a tear. Instead, raging with frustration, she slaps her dead husband's face three times. All the scenes of violence are quite gripping. The suspense preceding the death of Simon is built up flawlessly. On the other hand, the suddenness and savageness of Louise's death is genuinely shocking. Coppola does something else to intensify these sequences. Both sequences *seem* to reach their climax—only to be topped by a far more frightening climax. Swimming under water, Louise discovers the headstone that the others see only after the lake is drained. Horrified, she starts to climb out of the water, and is then bludgeoned to death. Simon discovers a replica of Kathleen and is still recoiling from this shock when the ax-wielder attacks again.

The film also proves that Coppola was justified in remaining pleased with the photography. There is not an abundance of camera angles (even later in his career, Coppola chose to work with few cameras), yet the camera work is never static, never dull. The camera angles that are presented are very effective ones. When Louise stares down at the annual funeral ceremony held in the garden on behalf of Kathleen, she is puzzled by this morbid ritual. The intricate design of the garden shrubbery reinforces her puzzlement.

Though predictable, the indoor settings are appropriate. Well-lighted rooms frame the cheerier family gatherings. Dimly lit passageways and dark rooms are used effectively for the scenes in which the mystery deepens. Finally, all the grisly shots are always thoroughly grisly, but never revolting—an achievement unmatched in many later horror films.

When the film opened in New York in 1963, however, it received very little attention from the critics. It was treated as fair game for derisive gags. Howard Thompson, writing for the *New York Times*, took the film somewhat more seriously and, in doing so, severely criticized it. He concluded, "Under the stolid direction of Francis Coppola, who also wrote the script, the picture stresses gore rather than atmosphere, and all but buries a fairly workable plot. William Campbell and Luana Anders head the unlucky cast."[35]

Other young men and women hungering to make a name for themselves as directors or scriptwriters may well have read the reviews and thanked their lucky stars *they* had not worked on exploitation films. Yet, despite the critical salvos aimed at *Dementia*

13, Coppola had gained invaluable filmmaking experience. In a relatively short time, he had worked as a film editor, soundman, production assistant, scriptwriter, and director.

Seven Arts

Interviewing Coppola after the release of *You're A Big Boy Now*, Joseph Morgenstern remarked that although Coppola certainly was a rebel, he nevertheless had gained the financial backing for his film from the conservative Hollywood Establishment. Coppola replied, "I pattern my life on Hitler in this respect. He didn't just take over the country. He worked his way into the existing fabric first."[36]

This comment raised a few eyebrows. Asked during another interview to elaborate on his analogy, Coppola said, "I was trying to say that as long as I believed in . . . film and filmmaking it didn't matter that I became part of the Hindenburg government, because I was going to make it my own. The way to come to power is not always to merely challenge the Establishment, but first make a place in it and then challenge, and double-cross, the Establishment."[37]

Prompted by this philosophy, and by his already-demonstrated willingness to compromise, soon after he returned from Ireland Coppola accepted a position as scriptwriter at Seven Arts (later Warner Brothers-Seven Arts). The offer of a job came after he won UCLA's 1962 Samuel Goldwyn Award for his screenplay *Pilma, Pilma*.

Yet, although aided by the film school, Coppola later spoke rather bitterly about his relationship with the school at this time. He never forgot the phrase that a fellow-student, hearing about Coppola's new position, wrote for him to see. "The day I got my first job as a screenwriter there was a big sign on the bulletin board saying: '*Sell out!*' Oh, yes, I'm the famous sell-out from UCLA." He said, "There was open resentment. I was making money. And I was sort of *doing* it. I was already doing what everybody was just talking about."[38]

In Coppola's opinion, one reason most of the students were not doing much was that the school's facilities were too limited. "When I attended UCLA, you were given a small amount of 8mm film, put out in a wheat field, and told to come back with a movie . . . . Gradually you would get to work with sound, although not with synchronized sound, and eventually you would move up to 16mm and learn to work with the Moviola. Finally, the instructor would pick two students out of the entire class and give them all the money that was available to film two student projects."[39]

There was also the matter of the students' naiveté. "The people at UCLA in 1960 who thought, 'I'm going to make a personal film about this thing that happened to me in Japan' refused to consider the fact that someone would have to put the money up for them to make their pictures." Summarizing his point, he said, "I think it is possible to make a very satisfying, important film that also makes money. That is the whole premise I work under."[40]

Any UCLA student who condemned Coppola's willingness to work for the Establishment must have chuckled more than once at what happened to Coppola in the first years of his connection with Seven Arts.

Coppola's first project was an adaptation of Carson McCullers' *Reflections in a Golden Eye*. "The company," Coppola recalled, "had bought the property but didn't know what to do with it. The executives were ready to drop the option, but because they already had so much money tied up in the project, they figured that they would move ahead with it if they could get someone young to work on it cheaply."[41]

The studio was impressed by Coppola's efforts and offered him a three-year contract. His beginning salary was $500 a week.

What happened to Coppola's script for *Reflections* was what happened to almost all the scripts he was to write for other people in the following years. It was drastically changed. Coppola once summed up the history of his scripts: "They finally got placed with a director and actors who brought in their own writers and nothing was used of them."[42] It is, therefore, fruitless to criticize Coppola's writing efforts with regard to the two films for which Seven Arts gave him (along with other writers) screen credits.

This Property Is Condemned is based on a one-act play by Tennessee Williams. In the play, Willie, a young girl dressed in "finery," walks along the railroad tracks, but then pauses long enough to tell a boy she meets about her sister Alva, now dead, and their mother's boarding house.

The film becomes an approximately two-hour elaboration of Alva's life. Played by Natialie Wood, Alva falls in love with Owen

Legate (Robert Redford in one of his several early screen appearances that made almost no impact on movie audiences at the time).
Alva's mother Hazel (Kate Reid) tricks Owen into believing that
Alva is unworthy of him; for Hazel wants Alva to marry someone
else. After Owen leaves town, Alva gains a momentary revenge by
marrying her mother's lover. She immediately jilts him, however,
and pursues Owen to New Orleans. Now it is Hazel's turn to gain
revenge. She sees to it that Owen learns about Alva's wedding.
Crushed, Alva turns promiscuous and, Camille-like, becomes
tubercular.

Bosley Crowther, writing for the *New York Times*, criticized the
screenwriters (Edith Sommer and Fred Coe were given screen
credit along with Coppola) for creating a "wholly implausible"
plot.[43] *Time* stated: "What condemns *This Property* is a plot tacked
on by the three zealous screen writers, to whom the Williams original 'suggested' a long, lurid flashback starring Natalie Wood."[44]
Hollis Alpert wrote one of the few not totally negative reviews. He
concluded that "all in all, [Tennessee] Williams is not badly
served."[45]

Years later, after he had worked extensively as both director and
scriptwriter, Coppola qualified his criticism of those who "do in" the
writer. He pointed out that a "screenplay, of course, is not a
finished piece of art; it's only the blueprint for a film. This becomes
clear when you direct from a script you've also written." He offered
an illustration. "After spending two months visualizing the female
lead as short and fat, you must be willing to dump her when you
suddenly find a tall, skinny actress who is better for the part." Then
he added, "The important thing is to go with the film and let it be
what it is—under your guidance, of course, and according to your
own intentions."

Nonetheless, Coppola still came to the defense of the writer.
"Most of the writers who share screen credits in Hollywood have
never worked together. One gets fired, and the other gets hired to
take his place . . . . It's like moving out of the house of the girl
you've been living with while the new guy is moving in. It's really
awful." He outlined the process. "A producer hires a writer to do
the first draft, and there is always something wrong with it because
first drafts are not finished drafts. So the producer says, 'Well, I
think he's shot his wad.' So he gets another writer who writes the
second draft—only it is *his* first draft. Finally, after seven writers,

the picture is shot with the seventh first draft—without ever having gotten to the second draft stage."

In sum, "The screenwriter's position is, in a word, impossible. Ridiculous. He gets a lot of money, but he has absolutely nothing to say about his film, unless he's one of the very few writers considered very important. This is particularly true for the young screenwriter."[46]

After his first year at Seven Arts, Coppola was given a raise. He now earned $1,000 a week. Yet his affluence brought him no contentment, not even after he had saved approximately $20,000. He said later, "I was really frustrated, because I could buy a Ferrari or I could buy a sailboat but I could not make a film."

He decided to go for broke. He took his $20,000 and played the stock market, hoping to turn his savings into a $100,000 jackpot that would enable him to have enough money to make a movie. He invested in Scopitone, centered on an invention—a jukebox with little films.

He lost his $20,000.[47]

Not long afterwards, Coppola received his next screen credit. It was for *Is Paris Burning?* Coppola later described his part in the production. "I had been sent to Paris by Seven Arts to accompany an elderly writer who was dying. I was to take the pencil from his hand when it fell out. This was going to be my great deal." After the writer died, Gore Vidal entered the scene. "Of course," said Coppola, "it was a junior-senior relationship. Vidal is a very bright guy, and he had it all figured out. He knew it was all a lot of baloney." Vidal's approach was to say, " 'Francis, yes,'—with that cigarette holder and all—'go back and figure out a scene for such and such, and I'll work on it.' He took it very casually."[48]

Coppola could not be that casual. He was deeply disappointed, and disgusted. "In the face of producer Paul Graetz, director René Clément backed down too often and the whole production backed down in the face of a government scared to okay a film that might displease Charles de Gaulle." What it came down to was: "There was really nothing to write about. You weren't even allowed to say the word 'Communist' in the script." In addition, "For some stupid reason, Clément's contract didn't give him a say over the script, and for some equally stupid reason Graetz wanted to keep it that way."

The situation became almost ludicrous. To outmaneuver Graetz, who blocked whatever Clément wanted, Clément and Coppola worked out a scheme. "Clément's ideas were presented as mine at story conferences, and of course I didn't mind, since Clément's ideas invariably were the best."[49]

The scheme was not enough to save the project. The film was a fiasco.

Based on the book by the same title written by Larry Collins and Dominique Lapierre, the film plot that finally emerged takes place in August, 1944. At this time, the French Resistance movement has succeeded in taking over part of Paris. The movement learns that the Allies are considering bypassing the city. Major Gallois is sent to convince the Allies to send some units into Paris. Meanwhile, General von Choltitz, the officer whom Hitler has put in command, ponders his leader's orders to burn Paris if and when the city can no longer be held. Because he does not want to be famous in history as the man who destroyed Paris, he disobeys Hitler's command. American and French fighters liberate Paris. (The French government was so satisfied with the slant of the final script that it freed the Place de la Concorde of all traffic one Sunday so that Seven Arts could film the liberation of Paris with style.)

Brendan Gill was obviously hesitant to crack down too hard on the scriptwriters. In his *New Yorker* review, he wrote, "Because it is plain that this ill-assembled botch is the work of many hands, nearly all of them working at clumsy cross-purposes on a kindergarten level of incompetence, I am sorry that, lacking private knowledge of how the innumerable sequences were shot and eventually Scotch-taped together, I am obliged to lay much of the blame for its failure on Gore Vidal and Francis Ford Coppola, the confessed authors of the grossly corny screenplay; I hope they will find some way of distributing appropriate shares of blame among their deserving colleagues."[50] Joseph Morgenstern, writing for *Newsweek*, also qualified his castigation of the screenwriters. He stated, "Incompetence, laziness or pressure from the producers led screenwriters Gore Vidal and Francis Ford Coppola to bulldoze the complexities of history."[51]

Bosley Crowther stressed a point others also emphasized. "In trying to stick to the nervous, episodic structure of the book, Gore Vidal and Francis Ford Coppola have come up with badly fragmented and bewildering continuity."[52] *Time* stated that "*Is Paris Burning?* is just possibly the most drastically disorganized war movie ever made. For one thing, the script tries to tell the story from about 60 points of view at once—some German, some American, some Free French, some Vichy French, some utterly unidentifiable."[53]

Although Coppola's career was to have a fair share of low points, this period was perhaps the lowest of all. Coppola considered his relationship with Seven Arts to be at an end. He owed the bank $10,000; and he had, now, a wife and two children to support.

Then one more blow came his way. When not working on *Is Paris Burning?* Coppola had written a script on his own, *You're A Big Boy Now*. Now he discovered that Seven Arts, pointing out that Coppola had done the writing on studio time, wanted to appropriate the script.

2

"So Let's Get Together"

You're a Big Boy Now

IT WAS 20th CENTURY-FOX that provided Coppola with the opportunity to climb out of his financial hole. The studio offered him $50,000 to write a screenplay based on the life of General Patton. It had already paid for other screen versions of Patton's life; and it would pay for still more versions. But, although Coppola would only gain fame as a writer of *Patton* several years later, his salary for the assignment freed him from immediate money problems.

He then returned to the project that vitally interested him—*You're A Big Boy Now*.

The *Big Boy* script originated from Coppola's desire to write a story about a teen-ager living in New York City. He was particularly intrigued by the fact that the young people working in the stacks in the huge New York Public Library on Fifth Avenue used roller skates to move rapidly up and down the aisles. (The definitive motion picture director, as opposed to theater director, almost always becomes interested in a story because of the visual images it evokes in his mind.) Well aware, however, that Seven Arts could appropriate any completely original screenplay he wrote, Coppola planned his strategy.

"I came across a novel titled *You're A Big Boy Now* by a young English writer named David Benedictus. It told the story of a nineteen-year-old kid who worked in a shoe shop, and there were so many similarities with my own screenplay that it seemed that we were both really writing about the same thing. So I bought the screenrights to the book myself, paying $1,000 for the option and $10,000 when the project was culminated, and fused my boy with his." Coppola explained, "I figured that although I was not allowed

43

Elizabeth Hartman (Barbara Darling) in You're a Big Boy Now
Credit: The Museum of Modern Art/Film Stills Archive

to own anything that I had written while I was with Seven Arts, I did own a property I had bought and paid for myself."

When Seven Arts declared that it owned the script of *You're A Big Boy Now*, Coppola was ready. "I told the company, 'I own the book on which the screenplay is based. Consequently, I own half, and you own half—so let's get together.' "

The producer appointed to handle *Big Boy* was Phil Feldman, an executive with whom Coppola had previously struck up a friendship. "After a good year of ups and downs and you-can't-do-it and you-can-do-it and if-you'll-sign-this and if-you'll-let-us-own-you-for-five-years and if-we-can-lend-you-out and if-you-can-make-it-for-$250,000, finally, after all that, we got permission to make it."[1] But the delay caused another problem. "By the time I got to make it, I didn't know whether I wanted to make it anymore. Because one of the great pities was that I had written *You're A Big Boy Now* before Dick Lester's *The Knack* came out and yet everyone said it was a copy. It was definitely influenced by *A Hard Day's Night*. But it was all there already before I even saw *Hard Day's Night*." He added, "One of the troubles of the film business is that you're always sort of forced to do things three years later."[2]

Casting the film proved still another obstacle. Coppola soon realized that he could not get a box-office star to play his film's "hero." Yet he very much wanted the film to be "a salable property." He decided to "cast all the other parts so that although no one name was an entity by itself, altogether the sum total of names did mean something, in a star sense."

Sans introductions, Coppola phoned Julie Harris, Geraldine Page, and Rip Torn and talked them into appearing in his film. He also signed up Elizabeth Hartman, Michael Dunn, Tony Bill, Peter Kastner (with one minor success to his credit, *Nobody Waved Goodbye*), and the then-unknown Karen Black. As a result, "Seven Arts was confident that it had the elements for a salable product that would minimize the financial risks it was taking and, in fact, was able to sell the film to television for a good part, if not most, of what it cost to make."[3]

Financial problems persisted, however. Although budgeted at $250,000 and made speedily under great time pressure, the film ended up costing approximately one million dollars. In fact, it lost money.

The scheme used to convince such performers as Rip Torn and

Julie Harris to appear in the picture was based on one premise. The actors were offered roles that were far removed from the usual type of characters that they had previously played. As Coppola commented, "Elizabeth Hartman, who is an attractive girl but certainly not a flamboyant one, played a very gassy go-go dancer. Peter Kasner [sic], a very sharp, bright kid, played the innocent boy. Tony Bill, who is the sweetest, most innocent kid you ever met in your life, played the pot smoker who knew everything about everything. Rip Torn, a young man in his thirties, played a fifty-year-old father."

Coppola got the idea for this approach from a story his father had told him. One day the Russian composer Prokofiev came to conduct the orchestra for which Coppola's father played the flute. "They rehearsed a piece of his that was very high and difficult. After the rehearsal, my father, a young man, went up to Prokofiev and asked him, 'Maestro, why did you write this part for flute when it is the range of the piccolo?' Prokofiev answered, 'Because I want you to strain for it.' "[4]

Coppola also had some unusual ideas about rehearsing the scenes in the film. He had come to believe that the system of rehearsing actors for films was totally inadequate. "In the theatre, the actor has sufficient rehearsal time to evolve a role to get it to a final performance level. But in film, the actor is called upon to hit his performance level for a given scene almost immediately."

Coppola decided to experiment. "To give the actors in the film a chance to develop their roles and to give myself the opportunity to visualize the film in its entirety, I tried a new method of rehearsal. I wrote two scripts. The first was very visual, describing essentially everything the film was trying to accomplish. The second—or rehearsal—script was intended to do the same thing in terms of dialogue rather than description." The cast concentrated on the second script. "We read it through, then began to block it out in a large room using boxes and whatever else was around for props."

This method helped Coppola at least as much as it did his cast; for, despite the film directing he had already done, he was still a novice when it came to directing a major million-dollar movie. But the system did help the actors, too. Coppola cited the example of Tony Bill, who "had a difficult time playing the dominant role in his relationship with Peter Kasner [sic]. Peter was so bright and hip that Tony was a little intimidated by him." To solve this problem,

Coppola "drew on the fact that Tony is a marvelous sailor and Peter doesn't know anything about sailing. We sat around for a day doing improvisations of Tony taking Peter out in a boat, and by the end of the day Tony felt confident that he knew more about something than Peter did. And Tony was able to make use of that confidence in developing his part."

The culmination of this kind of rehearsal experimentation came after a week and a half. "We played the entire script all the way through before a live audience. So we got the total flow of continuity that was essential if the actors were to evolve their parts and if I was to get a sense of what my picture was going to be like before we started shooting it."

Coppola then presented the actors with the shooting script. "Since the actual shooting script contained entirely different dialogue than the script the actors rehearsed with, they were able to start filming the picture with their characterizations and relationships fully evolved but with the freshness that comes from working with something brand new. Hopefully, we were able to get the best of both worlds."[5]

Even after all this, Coppola was very nervous when he began filming the script. "I didn't enjoy doing the film . . . . I was scared. My other experiences of directing plays and films had been very pleasurable. This time I was in New York and it was a real union crew, and I had a limited schedule."[6]

His nervousness quickly peaked. "The first day of actual shooting was a bit of a panic. There I was walking onto a set I had never seen before with nine actors and a crew of forty looking to me to tell them what to do. The photographer came up to me and asked, 'All right, where does the first camera go. What's the setup?' I had to answer that I didn't know . . . . Suddenly, I heard myself say, 'Okay, we'll stage it,' and forty-nine people were watching me to see if I knew what I was talking about. I started to get very nervous—desperate, really—and the crew had to leave for half an hour while I figured everything out."

A persistent difficulty was trying to figure out how to match action. "This is very simple in principle. For example, when you shoot a scene in which two actors are talking to each other and you shoot the first actor from over the shoulder of the second, you must change the camera direction when you shoot the second actor. Otherwise, the final result will give the impression that the two

actors are looking in the same direction rather than at each other."
But Coppola discovered that achieving the right result could be
very difficult when the scene takes place indoors. (This is why many
beginning directors—if they are shrewd—choose scripts filled with
outdoor scenes.)

"When you have nine actors turning and walking around," Coppola explained, "and *this* one is talking to *that* one and then to
another one, and the art director has put the door on *that* side and
the important area is over on *this* side, and you have to juggle
everything so that you can shoot a master and then shoot the closer
coverage so that it matches the master but doesn't cut into it, and all
the while the photographer is saying, 'I've been making pictures for
twenty years'—well, with all of this going on, matching action can
handcuff you terribly." Harried by this pressure, Coppola surren-
dered. He decided not to direct to match action. 'I figured that I
could get away with it so long as I shot the basic material I would
need to put the scenes together.'"[7]

When the actual filming ended, Coppola stayed in New York and
worked with the film editor, Aram Avakian. John Sebastian composed the songs including "Darling, Be Home Soon," (sung by
The Lovin' Spoonful) for the movie.

Like his short story "Candide—or Pessimism," Coppola's *You're
A Big Boy Now* is episodic in structure and focuses on a naive young
lad. Bernard Chanticleer first sees Barbara Darling when she comes
to the Fifth Avenue library where he and his friend Raef Delgrado
work. Bernard's father, I. H. Chanticleer, Director of Incunabula in
the library, calls Bernard into his office and declares, despite the
protests of Bernard's mother, who is also present, that Bernard is
now going to have his own apartment. This is his father's attempt to
help Bernard—finally—grow up.

It is quickly made clear that Bernard is not only pressured by his
father and by Raef, but also by the women in his life. In addition to
his mother, determined to keep Bernard tied to her apron strings,
there is his landlady Miss Nora Thing who, sexually repressed herself, wants Bernard to avoid sex. Another is Amy, who also works in
the library and who bumps into Bernard while he is wandering
around the Times Square area one night. And there is Barbara
Darling, whom Bernard sees again in Central Park, in a discotheque
where she dances, and in an off-Broadway play. After watching her
in the play, Bernard writes Barbara a fan letter.

Sexually assaulted when younger by a doctor whose artificial leg she steals and keeps as a trophy, Barbara is a man-hater. Probably for this very reason, she brings Bernard to her apartment and seduces him—except that, at the crucial moment, he becomes impotent. The next day, when Miss Thing goes to the library and complains about Bernard to his father, Mr. Chanticleer makes a pass at Miss Thing. Bernard senses what is going on and becomes totally disillusioned. Badgered by his parents, by Miss Thing and her policeman-boyfriend Francis Graf, and by Barbara and Raef (who succeeds with Barbara where Bernard failed), Bernard steals the library's famous Gutenberg Bible.

He is chased by all the others and finally knocked unconscious by Barbara with the leg of a manikin. In jail, Bernard is finally able to purge himself of the debilitating influence of his parents. So, when Amy puts up the bail money, Bernard, Amy, and Bernard's ever-faithful dog run jubilantly through the city streets and end up watching dough being shaped into pretzels in a pretzel factory.

Analysis

If judged too quickly, *You're A Big Boy Now* can appear to be little more than a structurally slapdash plot featuring stereotyped characters. It is true that the characters are based on stereotypes. And (as Joseph Morgenstern in *Newsweek* and Howard Thompson in the *New York Times* perceived) the plot does echo the episodic format used in Voltaire's *Candide*. [8] But if the viewer does not snap-judge the film, he will realize that, though basically stereotypes, almost all of the characters are individualized in enough little ways to prevent them from ever being dull. The viewer will also become aware that the film is tighter in structure than he first thought it was.

Consider, for instance, the structural metaphor of the cage. A few moments after the film begins, Bernard is in a cage that is part of the library's elevator system for transferring books from the stacks where Bernard works to the main desks from which the books are distributed to the public. Thus, when Bernard sees Barbara Darling for the first time, the cage literally cuts him off from her. Bernard soon sees Barbara several more times—in Central Park, at a discotheque, and in a play. But she always remains frustratingly out of reach. In a reversal of the metaphor, at the discotheque *she* is in a cage, a gleaming glass cage that dangles from the ceiling. In one of the movie's final—and most meaningful—scenes, Bernard is inside another cage, a jail cell. He now realizes that he has let his domineering parents confine him in a cage of guilt all his life. There is nothing structurally slapdash in this metaphor.

Although Bernard initially appears to be a young Casper Milquetoast, he does not, even at this early stage, completely fit this stereotype. It is against the rules for him to climb inside the elevator cage. Indeed, his friend Raef warns him off of it. Yet Bernard climbs aboard all the same.

The film, in fact, richly rewards the attentive viewer with its character delineations and plot developments. Very early, for example, Bernard calls Raef, "Ralph." His friend instantly declares that he wants to be called "Raef," for he seeks a new image of himself that the mundane name "Ralph" cannot imply. This is a quick signal that the film is going to focus on young people's search for their own identity and on their attempts to assert their individuality.

The signal is soon coupled with another one. Bernard's mother tries to name Bernard's dog "Rover." Bernard stubbornly rejects her repeated suggestion. He refuses to call the dog anything except "Dog."

Mrs. Chanticleer's desire to keep her son Bernard a baby is quickly established when she protests against her husband's decision to let Bernard have his own apartment. When mother and son leave Mr. Chanticleer's office in order to start searching for an apartment, Amy, a library assistant, gives Bernard a quick hello as he walks by. His mother, who never misses a thing, remains thoughtfully silent as they enter a taxi. Then she vigorously warns Bernard against being friendly with Amy. At Miss Thing's apartment house, Mrs. Chanticleer seizes upon the presence of a rooster in the hallway to condemn the building as unfit for Bernard. But when Miss Thing mentions that the rooster attacks girls, and only girls, Mrs. Chanticleer instantly decides the apartment is just right for her son.

Andy Laszlo's photography helps vivify the characters too. In a "free-association" sequence that occurs shortly after Bernard moves into his apartment, Bernard sees "Niggers Go Home" written on a subway billboard and asks himself where "home" is. He decides it is where the heart is. Where is the heart? In the highlands. And we

see his vision of a dancing string of black children following the
pied-piper lead of a black man playing the bagpipes. In this humor-
ous way, we realize that Bernard seriously seeks a definition of
"home."

The camera work cleverly conveys Bernard's uncertainty and lack
of direction as he, now living on his own, but merely lost and lonely,
wanders around the Times Square area. Glass partitions separate
him from the store goods he desires. (This visual effect foreshadows
his seeing Barbara dance—out of reach—in the glass cage.) Sexually
frustrated, he is tempted, but too timid to enter a dance hall. He
walks into a store containing pornographic magazines and postcards.
But raw sex, sex without love, repels him, though we do not realize
how completely until later, when Barbara offers him what amounts
to only sex.

He hurries out of the store, passes Amy without recognizing her,
and slips into another store that features sexy filmstrips. Just as the
film he watches nears its sexy climax, the machine becomes defec-
tive. On top of that, while he tries to rectify the problem, his tie gets
caught in the rolling cylinders.

Amy, who has trailed after him, comes to his rescue—as she will
again in the final sequence of the story. She "just happens" to have a
pair of large scissors with her and, without any ado, she cuts his tie
off. A simple bit of silent-movie-like comedy, the scene foreshadows
Amy's aiding Bernard later in more serious ways. That Amy aggres-
sively follows Bernard provides the first hint that it would be as
unwise to pigeonhole her as a passive person as it would be to label
Bernard as such.

This point is immediately followed up. Bernard blushes because
the subject matter of the filmstrip was sexual. But Amy makes it
clear that she "understands." What is surprising, and interesting, is
that she does understand. Right here, Amy parts company from the
stereotyped "nice girl." She, unlike Bernard, is not a "blushing
virgin." She may not even be a virgin. The night Bernard takes her
to the discotheque, Amy instantly perceives that Bernard is in-
fatuated with the go-go dancer in the cage above their heads and
forces him to leave. Outside, to regain his attention, she unshyly
kisses him. As the kiss ends, she coolly remarks that Bernard does
not "know anything."

She obviously does. She is quite willing to go to Bernard's apartment with him—much more willing than he is to take her there. It

is not only amusing that she is a very uninnocent "innocent girl," it also sets up the film's climax. (Bernard's final escape from all the domineering people who make his life miserable is rendered plausible by the fact that he is helped to escape by Amy, the aggressive sweet girl. She bails him out of jail.)

The next two sequences focus on Raef and Bernard. One of the things that prevents Raef from being a one-dimensional know-it-all has already been indicated—his nervousness about his name, his identity. Another is the wildly mixed bag of advice he gives Bernard. Some of his advice is goofy nonsense, some of it deliberately unhelpful. Yet some of it is quite good advice. While the two of them are flying a kite in Central Park, Raef tells Bernard, "Pain is part of freedom." This observation is something that Bernard fights off acknowledging, but finally admits is valid.

The kite breaks loose and floats away. This instigates one of the film's photographed-at-length "running sequences." There are far too many such sequences; and this one could certainly have been deleted. But the next sequence, centered on the discotheque, emphasizes another significant visual motif. In order to see Barbara dance, Bernard must look *up* at her. He had to do the same thing when he was crouched in the cage at the library. He had to do the same thing in Central Park where Barbara was sitting on top of a big boulder. Later, at her apartment, he is always physically situated in such a position that he must look up at her. This is capped by their scene on the bed. There, he is on the bottom; she hovers over him. The photography underscores Bernard's worship of Barbara, and her dominance over him.

The discotheque sequence is not without flaws, however. For one thing, a film-clip is shown on one wall of the restaurant, and it looks suspiciously like one of the grisly scenes in *Dementia 13*—a pointless private joke. A bigger problem is that the restaurant scene, psychedelic in effect, goes on much too long.

The pace quickens and the characters regain our attention when Amy pressures Bernard to take her to his apartment. Just as they reach his door, the rooster—all that Bernard's mother could hope for—attacks Amy. Alerted, Miss Thing, accompanied by Policeman Graf (the boarder who shyly admires Miss Thing), climbs toward the young couple. In the ensuing confusion Miss Thing loses her balance and falls down a flight of stairs. Amy is forced to retreat.

The next sequence focuses on Bernard and his parents. Bernard holds an umbrella over his father's head while the latter, despite the rain, practices his putting in his backyard and lectures his son. Mrs. Chanticleer, unwilling to let others influence her baby, doggedly shouts *her* views from the backdoor. Soon, chafing at the disadvantage of her distance from the men, she joins them in the rain. Later the three of them continue their verbal merry-go-round at the theater.

Mrs. Chanticleer is one of the few characters who does not clearly rise above a stereotype at some point in the story. What prevents this character from boring us is Geraldine Page. Even more than the other actors, Page brings an awesome zest to her role. The verve of all the acting is unquestionably one of the foremost virtues in the film, and Page leads the way. She makes her character crazily irresistible. Just Mrs. Chanticleer's screechy voice—no matter what the voice is saying—is continuously funny. It matches Olive Oyl's voice when she is beseeching Popeye to come to her rescue.

Mr. Chanticleer, on the other hand, is a subtle, ambiguous character. He treats Bernard like a slave. Bernard must get wet while protecting his father from the rain. Yet it is Mr. Chanticleer who insists that Bernard get his own apartment. It is left unclear, in an interestingly tantalizing way, just what the father's primary motives are. Certainly he is embarrassed by his son's ineptness. He does not want his awkward, bungling son embarrassing him at the place where they both work. He also does not want his son's naiveté to hinder his own extramarital sexual pursuits. Yet he does appear fond of Bernard.

Even Mr. Chanticleer's repeated use of the term "Big Boy" when referring to Bernard is ambiguous. Sometimes, he uses the phrase to prod Bernard to grow up. But sometimes he is needling Bernard, patronizing him. He stresses not the "Big" but the "Boy" part of the phrase.

Sneaky by nature, Mr. Chanticleer relishes his secret sex life. His name links him with the rooster Miss Thing owns. Both attack females. But the rooster wants only to injure them, while Mr. Chanticleer (cocky as Chaucer's famous Chauntecleer) wants to conquer them sexually. Although Bernard's innocence annoys or amuses Mr. Chanticleer, he finds the (apparent) innocence of Amy and the innocence-due-to-repression of Miss Thing sexually exciting. Locked in his vault with the fluttery Miss Thing, he is at first irritated. But as she begins to perceive the pornographic nature of much of his library collection of pictures, he finds this so exciting he is unable to resist trying a little hanky-panky with her, however imprudent the act may be.

Bernard's inability to figure his dad out is nicely dramatized early in the film. The son pauses to gaze at the sign outside his father's office. He studies the initials "I. H." and suddenly wonders what they stand for.

Yet Bernard takes his father at face value. He admires his father as the embodiment of the moral standards his father preaches to him. And he feels guilty every time he fails to live up to those standards. This is why Bernard is so intensely disillusioned when he discovers that his father is a fraud.

Barbara's character is spotlighted when Bernard mails his fan letter to her. Backstage at the theater, her only friend is a midget, who is writing a biography of her. Her conversation with the midget triggers a flashback. We learn that an albino doctor ardently pursued his desire to "examine" her. In revenge, and because of her own Barbara Allen nature, she ran off with his artificial leg and has kept it as a "trophy." After the flashback ends, she tells the midget that she hates all men's guts.

Curious, Barbara writes Bernard to tell him to come visit her. Now Bernard's women-problems begin to mount. He receives a letter from his mother, who is in the habit of mailing him locks of her hair. She considers him as her beau—in the most unexamined sense of the term. Miss Thing snatches Barbara's letter. She insists Bernard sit down and chat with her.

It is at this point that Miss Thing, in her turn, emerges as more than a one-dimensional character. She startles Bernard by stating that the two of them are alike. She is lonely and old; he is lonely and young. Immediately we suspect that she could be right. Her rambling monologue convinces us. Both Bernard and herself have been tyrannized and have become frustrated and repressed. Her nemesis was her now-dead brother. He interfered with her dates. He insisted on accompanying her everywhere. He gave her the rooster that hates young girls. He, in sum, warped her life.

This scene reenforces Coppola's main theme: We need to realize that the people we love and who love us are often our enemies.

Miss Thing, quite mellow now, gives Bernard Barbara's letter inviting him to meet her. This catapults Bernard into a state of euphoria. His mood is appealingly portrayed by one of the best of

the run-through-the-scenery sequences. The photography and
music blend successfully to delineate this lyrical moment in Bernard's life.

Only two flaws prevent the sequence from being totally successful. It goes on too long—another instance of Coppola's problems
concerning pace. Coppola also presses his point too hard. (He does
the same thing with the artificial leg. He repeatedly brings it back
into view, *and* has Barbara fondling a skeleton's leg bones in her
first meeting with Bernard, *and* has Barbara knock Bernard unconscious with the leg of a manikin.)

But the climax of this sequence is quite effective. Bernard loosens
his grip on the letter; and it glides away from him and down into a
sewer opening, an ominous ending concluded by another shot of
Bernard's face behind bars. He is seen mournfully looking through
the grate at the lost-forever letter.

The long and pivotal scene between Bernard and Barbara in her
apartment is a good one. Bernard is totally unsure of himself, so
Barbara has no trouble dominating him right from the start. She
slyly tells him to "relax," which doubles his nervousness. She insists
he ask her for a glass of milk, just as his overbearing mother
undoubtedly did in the past. Bernard obeys Barbara's commands
because he has been programmed to respond obediently to a woman's commands.

What this funny, yet poignant scene—and the subsequent scenes
involving Bernard and Barbara—also implies is that Bernard links
sex with love. He does not want to be a "virgin." But he wants sex to
be bred by love, though he is not consciously aware that he does. As
was true for the young hero in *Tea and Sympathy*, Bernard becomes impotent while with his "first woman" because a strictly
sexual "affair" chills his ardor.

Bernard sees a heart in a piece of artwork on Barbara's apartment
wall. He tenderly touches the heart—and a Murphy bed comes
down on top of him. Bernard never "touches Barbara's heart." He
arouses only her desire to use her bed—use sex—to humiliate men.

She becomes increasingly aggressive. She does not just undo
Bernard's shirt buttons. She rips them off. She tantalizes him by
dancing provocatively in front of him. She maneuvers him under-
neath her on the bed. Then she tells him she has a headache and
moves away. The next morning, she tells him not to be sad.

Miss Thing's statement that Bernard and herself are alike is soon
vividly dramatized. Key moments in the lives of both of them are

intertwined. The two start off in separate localities. Bernard is having breakfast in the automat with Raef. Worried about Bernard, Miss Thing goes to Mr. Chanticleer's office to inform him that Bernard has not been sleeping in his apartment. She thinks that Amy is the cause of this. But it is Mr. Chanticleer, not Bernard, who is preoccupied with Amy.

Mr. Chanticleer wants Amy to come "help" him in the vault. Amy makes herself unavailable. Miss Thing walks into the vault and, to ensure privacy, closes the vault door. It is at this time that Mr. Chanticleer cannot resist making a pass at Miss Thing.

Bernard arrives at the library. On his way to see his father, Amy stops him. Still trying to steer his attention to her, she tells him of his father's plot to entice her into the vault. The significance of this in relation to his reverent view of his father does not immediately dawn on Bernard. His first reaction is, "My poor mother."

Amy, more than a little miffed, replies, "Poor *me!*"

But Bernard simply proceeds into his father's office. There, the crash comes. Bernard sees Miss Thing, aided by a time-lock spring, fleeing from his father's sexual advances. It is a sad moment, a moment of deep disillusionment for a young man who has idolized his father and tried desperately to live up to his image of his father. Yet, in this moment, Bernard begins to win his freedom, despite the pain that is a part of freedom. He is freed from his simplistic view of reality. He no longer considers his father (and mother) as all-good and himself as hopelessly inferior, sinful.

Miss Thing is also liberated. (It must not be forgotten that her first name, "Nora," matches the name of the Ibsen heroine who turns her mousy life around too.) She has been forced (with a little subconscious help from herself?) to confront the monster Sex. Though shocked to her shoes, she has survived. In fact, she has become curious.

Staying close to her bed—because she is still so upset—she finally stirs her shy policeman-admirer to convey his feelings for her more openly. She hints—and hints and hints—to the cop about what Mr. Chanticleer tried to do. She succeeds in sexually arousing the cop a little, and in arousing herself quite a lot. So, she meets the policeman's tentative kiss more than halfway. The two fall on her old Victorian bed which, like these lovers' inhibitions, collapses.

Bernard continues to have his troubles. He has remained locked into his desire for Barbara. She continues to torment him. Utterly confused, he always proves impotent in bed. In anguish, he shouts,

"What's wrong with me!" Still seeking love as a framework for sex, he asks Barbara to marry him. Fortunately, Barbara is attracted to Raef, who comes to her apartment supposedly to inquire about Bernard, but actually to see what points *he* can score with this Barbara Darling he has heard so much about. Barbara sends Bernard on his way.

At this point Coppola "arranges" to have just about all the main characters converge on Mr. Chanticleer's office. Bernard's disillusionment and anger peak. He grabs the Gutenberg Bible and races out of the library, through the streets, and through Macy's store, where Barbara knocks him unconscious. It is difficult to guess how funny this chase scene would have been if it had not been preceded by so many similar scenes. While it was being filmed, it seemed to Coppola to be hilarious. Later, he, correctly, became disenchanted with the scene. It is simply too much of the same thing.

The ending of the film, however, consists of two satisfying twists. Raef, having succeeded where Bernard failed, has installed himself in Barbara's apartment. His self-confidence is soaring. But Barbara has gotten her name in the newspapers for halting Bernard's flight with the Gutenberg Bible. She finishes reading the papers, looks at Raef sprawled on her Murphy bed, and concludes that she is now too big a celebrity for the likes of him. He protests indignantly. And she literally sends him up the wall by kicking the bed so that it rises back into place.

Bernard, on the other hand, appears to have reached a dead end. He is in jail. But, instead of surrendering the struggle, he uses his time in the jail cell to think things over. He tells the nearby guard that his parents' influence on him caused him to be "filled with self-doubt, frustration, and perpetual guilt."

Bailed out, he leaves both his literal and symbolic cell. Prepared to face down his parents, he is surprised to discover that his benefactor is sweet Amy. She, in order to find out quickly whether she has wasted her money or not, wonders aloud if he is disappointed that it is not Barbara who has bailed him out. But he is free now of Barbara's influence too.

The lovers kiss.

Comparison with *The Graduate*

At the time when Coppola was considering making *You're A Big Boy Now*, he was offered $75,000 to write the script of a different movie. He so much wanted to make his own film, he turned down the other opportunity. He was paid only $8,000 to both write and direct *Big Boy*. "Why did I make *Big Boy* for just $8,000? Because that's what they could get me for. I would have done it for nothing."[9]

He hoped to profit financially from his film's box-office success, but the film failed to draw the crowds. It was completely overshadowed by *The Graduate*. The reasons for this are not difficult to find.

Although Peter Kastner did a fine job as Bernard, Dustin Hoffman was much more of a magnetic attraction as Benjamin Braddock. Nor did Coppola's film have any character as riveting as the now-legendary Mrs. Robinson (superbly portrayed by Anne Bancroft). There is no chance of the viewer snap-judging *The Graduate* as frivolous because, unlike *Big Boy*, it makes its serious side clear to the audience very early. It is a better-paced movie. It rarely overdoes a scene or repeats itself. It is further enhanced by Simon and Garfunkel's music and lyrics, vastly superior to the musical material in Coppola's film.

Yet a second viewing of both films reveals that the higher quality *overall* of the Mike Nichols movie is more apparent than real. *The Graduate* gives you nothing the second time that it did not give you the first time. In fact, a second viewing disappoints.

Only Mrs. Robinson remains interesting. Her daughter cannot compare with Amy who, in the skillful hands of Karen Black, is demure and bold, sweet and scheming, innocent and knowledgeable, honest and secretive. Benjamin is no more complex, no more intense, no more torn and twisted than Bernard. The rest of the characters in *The Graduate* are far nearer to being dull one-dimensional characters than the rest of the *Big Boy* characters. Coppola's script prevents Bernard's parents, Nora Thing, and Barbara Darling from sinking into dullness, and so do the rousing performances of the already-mentioned Geraldine Page and of Rip Torn, Elizabeth Hartman, and Julie Harris. Indeed, the mannerisms Torn gave Mr. Chanticleer—the shifty eyes, the half-smile, half-smirk on the lips, for instance—undoubtedly gave this character nuances beyond those provided in the script. Elizabeth Hartman's cool aloofness, her often deadpan expression as she says and does the most outrageous things to Bernard and Raef are perfect, saving Barbara Darling from being repellingly overbearing. Julie Harris shrewdly refused to make Miss Thing a shrinking violet.

Her Miss Thing is not only shy and sensitive, but vivacious and full of spunk. We fully accept that though Miss Thing is shocked by lecherous Mr. Chanticleer, she does not wilt. She retreats to her bed, but only to entice her timid lover into it.

The best scenes in *The Graduate* hold up well enough, but one waits impatiently for those few scenes. In *Big Boy*, there are good scenes *and* many clever touches all along the way. Finally, a comparison of the final sequence in each film clearly favors *Big Boy*. The climax of *The Graduate* is a cop-out. The young lovers have not really matured, have not really learned anything at all. In Coppola's film, however, Amy is wise even before Bernard becomes interested in her; and Bernard, by the time the film ends, has learned much about others and about himself, and has matured in the process. Bernard and Amy run away in order to build on the foundation of what they know. Their counterparts in *The Graduate* simply run away.

Nonetheless, *The Graduate* brought Mike Nichols still more fame and fortune. *You're A Big Boy Now* brought Coppola a few complimentary reviews—and many negative ones.

3

"If The Vision Is Right"

Finian's Rainbow

COPPOLA USED *You're A Big Boy Now* to fulfill his graduate-school requirements for a thesis. He rented an office and began to write another screenplay, the first pages of a rough draft of what eventually became *The Conversation*. Then the telephone rang.

"I got a phone call from a guy who asked if I knew anyone who could do *Finian's Rainbow*," Coppola recalled. "I thought about it and gave him some suggestions and hung up."

The next day the man called again and said, "What about you?"

And, although Coppola had vowed not to reenter the Big Studio world until he could deal from a position of power, he accepted the offer.[1]

During interviews in later years, Coppola cited some of the reasons he accepted the offer. His father had been in the musical comedy business at various times, and Coppola thought, "Wouldn't my father be happy if I did a big musical?"[2] As he recalled, the musical, first staged in 1947, had a first-rate score and was "a lovely old show" with "something warm about it. And I thought that maybe if I could do it right, that if I could find the balance, I could make it timeless . . . . I had always loved musical theater."[3]

Coppola's initial enthusiasm was soon dealt a severe blow. He read the play. Immediately he knew that the book would not do at all. He considered the plot ridiculous. Worse, the play's stance on civil rights, though liberal in its day (twenty-one years in the past), was outdated.

He rewrote parts of the story, although his name does not appear in the credits for the screenplay. He rehearsed and began filming the show. Both he and the people at Warner Brothers-Seven Arts wanted the pace of the musical to be fast and lively—as was the pace

61

Fred Astaire (Finian McLonergan) in Finian's Rainbow

in sections of *You're A Big Boy Now;* and he tried to achieve that kind of tempo. Yet he did not want to "get fancy," as he phrased it. He wanted to give the picture "a lot of warmth and affection."

Coppola said later, "If you look at the chorus during this movie you'll see lots of miscues or flutterings. As you know, kids are very hard to program. And the more you get kids that are programable, the more phony they are. Also, there wasn't lots of time to keep going after every detail. Very often I was going for what I felt was the essence of a scene. I always feel a director directs his movie before it's even done. If the vision is right, then you'll forgive a lot of this other stuff. More time will help alleviate the rough details. But I feel if the audience didn't enjoy it, it's because of the vision." He also commented, "I would shoot a scene eight times. And it would be different every time. And then I'd jump-cut mismatched bits together. In other words, I'd never try to match the picture."[4]

Despite the lingering optimism Coppola still felt, and despite the soaring optimism of the studio heads, production troubles developed. In an interview with Joseph Gelmis Coppola spoke at length about these problems. There were only three and a half weeks of rehearsals, followed by twelve weeks of actual shooting. Because the shooting went so rapidly, and because of other problems, Coppola was soon out of all the material he had prepared. From then on, Coppola admitted, "I was faking it."

One of the other problems was the choreography. "I wanted to do the musical numbers. I dreamed up the way the numbers were going to be done. I said, 'Grandish.' I'll shoot it on a hill and have Petula Clark hanging white bed sheets. And 'If This Isn't Love' will be done with children's games. And 'On That Great Come And Get It Day' they're going to throw away all their old furniture in big piles." He had a basic idea for every musical number. The problem was the choreographer.

Coppola needed a choreographer to create the dance-step routines. But he quickly came to believe that the choreographer assigned to the production—a man hired "at Fred Astaire's insistence"—was "a disaster." Thus, the "choreography was abysmal . . . . We fired the choreographer halfway through the picture." Once again, Coppola had to resort to "faking it."

Coppola cited an example. "After the song 'If This Isn't Love' we were supposed to go into a big production number. Well, it was so awful that I finally got little Barbara Hancock (Silent Susan, in the film) and we went back and I shot her with a 500-mm lens going in and out of the trees. She was just faking it. And that's the way the numbers were done."

Nor was Coppola happy with some of the actors' approaches to their roles. He said bluntly to Gelmis, "Don Francks never did improve, as an actor." He had even more problems in his working relationship with Tommy Steele. "I think I could have done better with him. When we were doing the rehearsal, Tommy was doing his *thing*. And I said to him that I really felt we were going in the wrong direction. Everyone loved him and told Tommy he was so great. But I felt the leprechaun should be more shy and timid and bewildered. When I first came into the picture, I wanted Donal Donnelly to play the part. I wanted it to be an introvert leprechaun, a guy who speaks in this quiet voice and then suddenly becomes a human being."

Coppola tried to keep this idea alive. "At my insistence Tommy started to do just that in the rehearsal, and he really was good at it. But actors are funny people. They have certain crutches that they rely on. And they're very unwilling to let those crutches go when they feel insecure. And somehow during the actual shooting, little by little, he slipped back into his familiar character."

Coppola did not perceive the change. "You don't notice it because you're shooting little pieces. And that's the whole game of directing. Directing takes a lot of concentration and being able to be blind to certain problems and just focus where you should be focusing. I did that in some cases. In some cases I failed. With Tommy, I wanted a different kind of performance and he eluded me."[5]

Perhaps the biggest problem of all, however, was that Coppola was working within the walls of a big studio for the first time. He was in charge of a multimillion dollar production, and he was not at all sure of the lay of the land. He was not at all sure that what he saw as serious problems were in fact serious problems.

Later he commented that he was working "in a methodology I didn't understand very well and over which I had no control. I'd express some doubts about the way things were going, and the people around me would say, 'It's going great.'" He added, "We had no sour notes on *Finian's Rainbow;* everyone kept saying how terrific everything was all the time." When the movie was savaged by the critics, Coppola remembered this steady stream of reassurance and unqualified praise with more than a little bitterness. Dryly, he described his current approach to working on a production. "I try to work with people who won't hesitate to say, 'We're making a mistake.' "[6]

Nevertheless, Coppola had a great deal of power during the filming of *Finian's Rainbow*, enough power to make it quite fair for the audience to praise or condemn him for the quality of the film. Coppola himself stressed the amount of authority he had. He stated, "I had my way, within the limitations of time and money. I was very responsible."

Something that Coppola had no control over, however, was the way *Finian's Rainbow* was presented to the public. In terms of the types of movie musicals then being produced, *Finian's Rainbow* was not originally intended or ever budgeted to be a "roadshow" musical. These were shown in big theaters only twice a day at higher-than-usual, "hard-ticket" (reserved seat) prices. It was not an expensive film compared to the big roadshow musicals of the time, such as *Funny Girl* and *Star!* These shows cost approximately ten million dollars each. *Finian's Rainbow* cost $3,500,000.

Coppola later elaborated on what became another sore point. His picture "was made on the Warners' back lot, the 'jungle.' I shot just eight days out of the studio. The location footage was carefully interspersed in the film and used with the titles." Compared to the less-than-four-weeks rehearsal time he had, Herb Ross rehearsed the *Funny Girl* numbers for a far longer period of time. *Finian's Rainbow* "was shot in twelve weeks while *Star!* was made in six months."[7]

Yet—and this was the rub—the studio heads, Coppola declared, "decided to blow the picture up to 70 and make it a roadshow picture. And when they did that, they blew the feet off Fred Astaire when he was dancing. No one had calculated the top and bottom of the frame."[8] It was advertised as if it had been designed and produced as a roadshow musical.

Harsh comparisons inevitably followed—harsh, that is, as far as *Finian's Rainbow* was concerned.

As the movie begins, Finian McLonergan and his daughter Sharon, having left Ireland, are wending their way to Rainbow Valley, Missitucky. Just when they arrive, bigoted Senator Rawkins attempts to seize the property where whites and blacks live together peacefully and where Woody, a white, and Howard, a black scientist, own a laboratory. Finian helps pay the taxes so that Rawkins

cannot take the land. Woody and his neighbors give the McLonergans some of the land. Finian buries a pot of gold (which he stole
from Og, a leprechaun) near Fort Knox, for he believes it will
multiply in that soil.

Woody and Sharon fall in love. She learns that Woody and Howard are trying to develop a mint tobacco plant that will burn. So far
unsuccessful, Howard has to work for Rawkins in order to obtain
money for his experiments. Meanwhile, Og, who is gradually changing into a human being, has pursued the McLonergans to Missitucky in an attempt to retrieve the gold because he knows that if
he does not find it, he will continue to change into and then remain
a human being.

When geologists discover the presence of the pot of gold, Rawkins tries again to seize Rainbow Valley. The gold has the power to
grant three wishes; when Sharon wishes that Rawkins were black so
that he could better understand them, her wish is granted. Sharon
is then condemned to burn as a witch. Og, knowing about the gold's
power, uses up the last two wishes. Having fallen in love with
Woody's mute sister, Susan the Silent, he uses the second wish to
bring her the power of speech. He must use the third wish either to
save Sharon by turning Rawkins back into a white man or to become
a leprechaun again.

Susan kisses Og, and he decides to be a mortal. His third wish
rescues Sharon. The gold turns to dross, but the fire that was started
to burn Sharon reaches Howard's newest mint tobacco plants—and
burns them. Now the Rainbow Valley people have no money problems. Woody and Sharon marry. And Finian decides to travel on
down the road.

Analysis

Years later Coppola was still pondering whether his approach to
the plot of *Finian's Rainbow* had been the correct one or not. "I had
the idea," he remarked, "that if you do *Finian's Rainbow*, you
shouldn't rewrite it and update it. I guess I was wrong." He added
that "it was just the wrong time to make a movie like that."[9]

That the plot is weak, thin, is an inescapable fact. Nor can it be
denied that the mood of an era plays a vital role in whether a movie
or play will please its audience or not. The Alan Bates' vehicle *King
of Hearts*, a fragile anti-war comedy, came and went quickly when

it was first presented in American movie theaters. Revived at the height of the Vietnam War protests, it ran for well over two years in one Boston movie house alone. When *Finian's Rainbow* opened on Broadway, January 10, 1947, war-weary audiences were immediately charmed by its good-hearted, though simplistic liberal attitude toward racial problems. Too much happened in the following twenty-one years to allow a 1968 audience to react to the film version in the same way.

Yet the main problem with a film version of *Finian's Rainbow* is not that it totally depends for success on a certain political mood prevailing at the time the picture is released. The main problem is that the plot is basically whimsical. Whimsy is much easier to create and sustain in a play than it is in a movie. A movie house's big screen, to state the obvious, makes everything shown on that screen super-real. Fantasy can be successfully offered to a movie audience, but it must be presented within a very clearly defined framework, and with enormous skill.

When a plot is simultaneously somewhat realistic and yet basically whimsical, it is going to have a great deal of trouble gaining acceptance from a movie audience. Movie audiences want what they see to be clear-cut, stark, and realistic. They do not expect to put their imaginations to work to any serious degree, and they will not do so. They expect the camera work and the background music and the big screen to intensify the plot for them. In theater, the overwhelming majority of plays staged during the centuries were not realistic in style. The theater audience expects to use its imagination in order to be drawn into the action—whatever the style devised to present that action is. A theater audience will readily accept many, many things, including whimsy. So, too, whatever advantages a film actor has over a stage actor, it is easier for a stage actor with personal magnetism to charm and beguile a live audience into accepting a whimsical plot premise.

In fairness to Coppola's *Finian's Rainbow* it should be pointed out that, although the film is a failure, there are some nice things in it. The musical score that Coppola had remembered as being captivating is indeed so. Four songs in the film are rendered in delightful fashion. "Look to the Rainbow," featuring Petula Clark and Fred Astaire, is one of the film's first big production numbers and the best of them. The music and lyrics lend themselves equally well to the alternately fast and slow tempo. "Something Sort Of Grandish" receives a spirited delivery. Although Tommy Steele presses too hard, Petula Clark is a joy to watch and listen to. Coppola's idea of using a hilltop filled with laundry—on and off the clotheslines—as a backdrop for the song was a lovely idea.

Juxtaposed in the first half of the film to the verve and speed of these two numbers is the quiet presentation of "How Are Things In Glocca Morra?" and "Old Devil Moon." Petula Clark shines in the first number shortly after the film begins. She does an equally pleasing job singing the second song, though here she is somewhat hampered by Don Francks, who sings with her.

Al Freeman, Jr. (Howard) and Keenan Wynn (Senator Rawkins) should also be singled out for praise. Wynn is irascible, but funny as the wildly greedy and bigoted Rawkins. His best scene is his first, a scene in which he combines with Freeman to give the audience a gem of a comic sketch, the only sustained funny scene in the film. Rawkins expects his black servants to be lazy and slow-moving; and Howard pretends to fit that stereotype just at the time Rawkins wants speed-speed-speed.

The first half of the film contains a few other funny moments. But the problems in the first half overlap with the bigger problems in the second half to undercut and finally spoil the movie far more than its weak plot does. Except for Freeman and Wynn and Petula Clark's performance while singing, the acting is poor. Fred Astaire is completely miscast. As anyone familiar with the Astaire-Rodgers musicals knows, Astaire can play the sophisticate (such as a Broadway hoofer), but he cannot play a "whimsical Irishman." In *Finian's Rainbow* Astaire delivers his few funny satirical lines flawlessly. Otherwise, he is embarrassing. To no small degree, the successful creation of a whimsical atmosphere depends specifically on the Finian character (more so, even, than on the leprechaun). Astaire's inability to create a convincing Finian is an important reason the film fails.

The scenes featuring Astaire and Tommy Steele (as Og) are particularly poor; and the fault is by no means all Astaire's. Steele's portrayal of Og is as big a mistake as Coppola said it was. Steele overacts. His singing voice is monotonous, his mannerisms boring. Unlike Astaire, who is never allowed to utilize fully his one great talent—his ability to dance, Steele is given all sorts of comic and melodic opportunities. And he bungles every one.

Barbara Hancock, in the role of Susan the Silent, is given even less opportunity than Astaire. She just keeps on twirling her skirt, hour after hour. As Woody, Don Francks turns in the poorest acting job of all. He is wooden from his first moment in front of the camera to his last. He gives the kind of performance that permits the critic who loves to compose nasty funny gibes an ample opportunity to do so.

Yet to put all the blame for the film's failure on the weak and whimsical plot and on the actors would be very unfair. Coppola himself stressed his responsibility for the dismal performance turned in by Steele. He is at least partially responsible for all the other bad performances. He also muffed the opportunity offered him in the character of Susan. In the play, her character— dramatized most by the "messages" she conveys in her impromptu dances—helps nurture the "magical" atmosphere of Rainbow Valley. She is attuned to nature and to the supernatural. Along with Finian and Og, she links the whimsical with the realistic. Coppola's film gives us none of this. Coppola presents us merely with a sweet—bland—Susan.

Shortly after the film was released, Coppola stated that he tried to achieve his effects in a subtle way so that the film "wouldn't come out like what they did to *A Funny Thing Happened on the Way to the Forum*."[10] Anyone who has seen Richard Lester's *Forum* (1966) and Coppola's musical knows that Coppola's statement is sheer balderdash. Allowed entry because Coppola wanted a fast pace, Lester's influence is all too present. As was the case when he made *You're A Big Boy Now*, Coppola in *Finian's Rainbow* is particularly attracted to Lester's fondness for a fast-unto-pell-mell pace and running-through-the-scenery sequences. *Big Boy* is hurt by this influence. *Finian's Rainbow* is maimed by it.

The pell-mell pace of some of the early sequences in *Finian's Rainbow* is acceptable. The razzmatazz in three production numbers, "This Time of the Year," "Look to the Rainbow," and "Something Sort Of Grandish," is done well on the whole—and, of course, is the *first* razzmatazz in the film. It is also contrasted by the lovely quieter numbers such as "Old Devil Moon."

But as the film goes on, the continued, almost relentless run-run-running becomes first tedious and then numbing. Even the potentially charming scene in which Astaire entices the children of Rainbow Valley to run around looking for the now-lost pot of gold is tedious because of all the running that has preceded *this* running.

For the same reason, the picnic sequence revolving around "If This Isn't Love" is tedious. Before this number ends, Susan, having already run and twirled her skirt countless times, is placed on a galloping horse. The hyperactivity of all the Valley people while singing "The Great Come-And-Get-It Day" and joining Astaire in rendering "When the Idle Poor Become the Idle Rich" appears to be just a desperate attempt to top all the running done in the previous numbers. Apparently Coppola then felt that the only way to top all *that* was to present "Begat" in what seems to be an endless number of shots of the singers fixing their car, pushing the car, and drive-drive-driving the car.

Perhaps the core of Coppola's problems while making *Finian's Rainbow* was that he was simply in over his head. His belief that if a director's "vision is right," all his mistakes will be overlooked—a belief expressed while *Finian's Rainbow* was opening in theaters across the nation—sounds more like a fervent hope than a firm conviction. Coppola, on the set, was indeed, as he himself said, "faking it."

Of course, given all the unforeseeable things that occur while a movie is being made, every director on every set is "faking it" in the sense that he is ad-libbing solutions to problems and hoping for the best. Sometimes he is lucky, and his intuitions help provide him with the right solutions. But good intuitions are only one tool a director must have, and even intuitions are at least partially based on experience. Coppola had very little experience as a director before he made *Finian's Rainbow*.

He also admitted that he quickly ran out of the material he had thought through ahead of time. His preparations for making the film were inadequate. Nor did he really have an overall "vision" of his musical. However weak the plot was, Coppola did not utilize the potential residing in the material; for he had no clear, detailed, viable idea of how to utilize it.

4

"I'll Write You A Movie"

WARNER BROTHERS was positive that when *Finian's Rainbow* was released, it would prove to be a big hit. The studio offered Coppola $400,000 to direct another musical, *Mame*. Coppola, however, began to have doubts about the musical he had just completed.

His lack of self-confidence intensified. He wondered if he were postponing writing a serious original screenplay and directing it because he did not really have the ability to do so. He began to fear that he did not have the talent he once thought he possessed.

He decided to permit no more postponements. He would force a confrontation with himself. He turned to a project he had already considered doing—filming *The Rain People*. Using money he had earned for directing *Finian's Rainbow*, he bought $80,000 worth of movie equipment. He also helped to support financially the *Rain People* cast and crew. (One member of the crew was George Lucas, a young University of Southern California graduate whose film career would be intertwined with Coppola's for several years.)

Coppola ended up spending all the available money he had, but he still could not come near covering the expenses for making his film. This was when the esteem Warner Brothers had for him came to his aid. Warner Brothers agreed to bankroll *The Rain People*.

The Rain People

The story that evolved into *The Rain People* originated while Coppola was at Hofstra College. "It was first called *Echoes*," he recalled, "and it was the story of three housewives—a newly married one, an older woman, and one who has a few kids. All go off in a station wagon and leave their husbands. I wrote it for a creative writing class." However—and this turned out to be a very important

71

point concerning the making of the film—Coppola never finished that story.

Several years later Coppola became an admirer of Shirley Knight's acting talent. He also resumed an old habit—fantasizing. "The idea of writing a film for an actress and making it together, like Antonioni and Monica Vitti, really appealed to me." Then Coppola met Knight at a film festival. "She was crying because someone had been rude to her . . . . I went up to her and said, 'Don't cry, I'll write you a movie.' And she said, 'You will? That's sweet.' "

Whether Shirley Knight took Coppola seriously or not, he did as promised. "I took out this old college draft and decided to make it just one character."[1]

Coppola later elaborated on the development of the screenplay. "What it really comes down to is a pregnant woman, sitting in a car, literally walking out on all the responsibilities one associates with a young wife. And putting distance between herself and that." Her act is the result of her whole marital situation. "She gets married and suddenly starts feeling her personality being eroded, not knowing why. What is she supposed to perform in this thing, marriage? What's her place? A lot of women have a terrible time with this. And she's pregnant. That's the final straw."

The actual filming started out swimmingly. It was "a labor of love," recalled Coppola. "We had a very small crew in a remodeled Dodge bus that we rebuilt ourselves and filled with the most advanced motion picture equipment available."[2] The film was shot in sequence. "I was writing it while we were shooting it. It wasn't pre-scouted. We just drove." When he saw a setting he liked, he stopped. "The big parade sequence in Chattanooga, we literally just came across."

Soon, however, serious trouble occurred. "I started having tremendous arguments with Shirley Knight. She's very talented, but she's the only actor I really haven't gotten along with. Usually I get along with actors." The crux of the trouble, in Coppola's opinion, was a matter of trust. "I don't think Shirley Knight trusted me. I don't think she felt that if she did what I asked her to do it would be a good movie."

The arguments centered on the interpretation of Knight's character in the film. Coppola said, "The character as I had written it had a lot of the schizophrenia that comes out in the film, but there was also a tremendously compassionate side. The whole basis of the

character was that she was a mother, a mother figure. And I didn't
feel that I was getting that from Shirley. I would get the high-
strung, nervous intensity. I don't know how much I liked that
·character I saw, whereas I liked the character I had written."
    Because Coppola was writing the script as he went along, his
arguments with his leading lady led him to alter his original idea for
the plot. "I started to throw more weight to Jimmy Caan's character.
That is definitely the flaw in the film." He admitted: "I chickened
out, partly because I didn't have enough time. When a writer
doesn't know what else to do with a character, he brings in a new
character . . . . So I kept bringing in new, interesting characters,
like the cop or the animal farmer, hopefully keeping the audience
interested but denying what I should have been doing, which is to
explore that main premise."
    Later, he came more and more to regret the opportunity he lost
while making the movie. For he was very interested in a woman's
viewpoint on issues large and small, impersonal and personal, long
before the women's liberation movement began clamoring that
more attention be paid to that point of view. He said later, "I think
I've always been empathetic enough to put myself in a woman's
place, although they say it's impossible." He added, "I felt that
there must be women who are married and expected to perform in a
certain way who are really dying on the inside. I thought it was an
interesting statement, that a woman could just wake up and leave."
    Coppola was also fascinated "by the idea of the responsibility that
we have to one another." His main character went on a trip precisely to avoid responsibility, and then gave a lift to a mentally-
maimed male "who's a metaphor for her baby that she's pregnant
with. It's like a woman driving in the car and having a discussion
with this kid who isn't born yet, saying, 'I really can't be responsible
for you, I've got to take care of myself.' At the same time she feels a
very definite instinctive attachment to him."
    But, Coppola admitted, "I never really said, 'What does all that
mean? Does that mean that woman is destined, through her biologi-
cal make-up, to be at home with her husband?' I don't know if that's
what it means, but I wish the film had answered that." In his own
opinion, the film's ending is a bit of a cop-out. "I ended the movie
with a *deus ex machina* and a very emotional plea to have a family."
    Coppola disagreed, however, with the women in his audience
who thought he was merely saying—like many another male—that a

woman should stay home and have babies. For him, the final emphasis was intended to focus on the concept of family, a concept that
the male as well as the female should honor and adhere to. "I'm
fascinated with the whole idea of a family. In the things I'm writing
that is constant."[3]

Natalie Ravenna is the name of the character Shirley Knight
plays. Living on Long Island, Natalie wakes up one day, writes a
note to her husband that she is leaving, and drives off. She stops
briefly to talk with her parents and then heads west. While in New
Jersey, she phones her husband (for the first of several times) and
informs him that she is pregnant, that she feels trapped by her
responsibilities, and that she must get away until she can come to
some firm decisions.

The next day, she picks up Jimmie Kilgannon. He was a college
football star, but an injury rendered him slightly mentally retarded
and necessitated his wearing a metal plate in his head. The college
gave him $1,000 and asked him to leave. He tells Natalie that he will
find work with his former girl friend's father.

It turns out that the family wants no part of Kilgannon. Disgusted
with the family, Natalie tells Kilgannon to get back in the car. Some
time afterwards, while delayed by a parade, Natalie decides to leave
Kilgannon, but at the last minute, she changes her mind and takes
him with her again. After they have driven on a good distance, she
hesitantly arranges for Kilgannon to work as a handyman in a small
zoo run by sleazy Mr. Alfred.

Upset, she drives away so fast that she is given a speeding ticket
by a policman, Gordon, who quickly becomes personally interested
in her. Mr. Alfred is the local justice of the peace. When Natalie
returns to his place to pay the fine, she discovers that Kilgannon has
released most of the animals in the zoo. The two are forced to give
the angry Mr. Alfred most of Kilgannon's money.

Frustrated and furious, Natalie bids goodbye to Kilgannon and
turns her attention to Gordon. Gordon takes her out for the evening
and then brings her to his trailer-home, where he lives with his
daughter Rosalie. When he becomes too ardent and insistent,
Natalie pushes him off. Outside, Rosalie meets the roaming Kilgannon and returns with him to the trailer. Kilgannon becomes enraged
at Gordon's rough behavior and charges at him. Rosalie, fearful for
her father, gains possession of his revolver and shoots Kilgannon.

Natalie, sobbing, pulls the dying Kilgannon away; all the while, she promises him, "I'll take you home and we'll be a family."

Analysis

When first seen, Natalie is in bed with her husband Vinny. He, though asleep, has one arm draped over her body; he is literally pinning her down. She pushes free of him, dresses, and prepares to leave. Yet before she closes the front door behind her, she sets Vinny's place at the breakfast table. This act makes it clear that even at the moment she is about to run off, even at this emotional highpoint, Natalie is not really a reckless, free-spirited individual.

She stops off to see her parents, who soon begin to bicker. She cannot unburden herself to them. She stops along the highway to phone her husband; and she tells him that she wants to be free, that it used to be that her day was *hers*—but now it is *his*. She tells him that she is pregnant, but that although she loves him, she must get away for a while. Then she heads west.

This opening is well done. The camera work captures all the scenes' nuances. The pace, appropriately, is swift, the acting taut. Yet very quickly a problem emerges, for these scenes breed questions that are never answered.

Except in the broad terms indicated by her phone conversation, we do not know how to interpret Natalie's flight from home. It may be the act of an intelligent, sensitive woman, or it may be the act of a sadly neurotic woman. It may be as heroic as Nora's departure in *A Doll's House*. It may be a spoiled brat's act. All that we vaguely know is that Natalie, like many other women (and many men), feels that marriage restricts her individuality, and, like some other women (and some men), she runs away from this pressure.

Flashbacks are soon employed. But—a serious flaw in the film—they do not clearly delineate the life Natalie and Vinny shared nor define what specifically in that relationship rubbed Natalie the wrong way. In contrast, for instance, in the opening scenes of *Diary of a Mad Housewife*, the audience quickly learns all it needs to know about the main characters' married life.

The flashbacks offered while Natalie drives and while she is alone in a motel room present no pertinent information. This weak spot in the film is made still weaker by Coppola's decision to employ far too

much "travelogue photography." Instead of information, the film
gives us pretty scenery—long after it is made clear that Natalie is
driving west. The "travelogue photography" is also the first instance
of a recurring problem in the film: its pace is often too slow.

This first segment of *The Rain People* proves indicative of the
whole movie. It is an extremely uneven film. There are individual
scenes that are as good as the best work Coppola achieved in his
finest films. Natalie and Kilgannon (played by James Caan) become
thoroughly interesting characters. And, to the degree that it is concentrated on, the theme of the movie is a powerful one. But *The
Rain People* ultimately proves disappointing. Just as Coppola came
to believe, it promises more in thematic terms than it delivers.
Serious flaws undercut some sequences and cripple others. Coppola's attempt to ad-lib much of the plot while he and his entourage
roamed the country is, finally, an attempt that does not succeed.

Though flawed, the next sequence, when Natalie and Kilgannon
first meet, is a good one. That Natalie stops for Kilgannon, then
starts to drive away before he can enter the car, then stops again and
lets him enter is dramatically incisive. Her actions highlight her
basic uncertainty. The night before, alone in her motel room,
Natalie thought more than a little about sex. She will tell Kilgannon
she had been thinking about what it would be like to "make it" with
someone other than her husband. Still, when she spots Kilgannon,
she is not positive she wants to implement her fancy.

Ironically, whether she picks up a hitchhiker or not seems a
minor question to her in comparison with the major question of
what is she going to do with the rest of her life. Yet by the time
Kilgannon dies, in the not too distant future, Natalie's relationship
with this hitchhiker is completely entangled with that major question.

That night, while Natalie methodically applies makeup in prep-
aration for her night of sex with Kilgannon, a radio next to her elbow
features the Gershwin lyrics "They're writing songs of love, but not
for me." This provides a further irony. Natalie, unlike the personae
of the song, does not pine for or seek love. She seeks to escape its
complications. She wants only to enjoy her new sexual freedom. But
the "casual affair" she is instigating will lead her, however reluc-
tantly, to love Kilgannon.

Because it is already apparent that Kilgannon is a little "slow,"
Natalie appropriately resorts to a children's game in order to ma-

neuver this "child-man" toward the sex she wants from him. They play "Simon Says" (in which one player is not supposed to carry out the other's request unless it is prefaced by "Simon says"). She soon has this docile stud literally on his knees in front of her. It appears that her impulse to pick a man up in her car has brought her a man who will do whatever she wants while entangling her in no serious way at all.

But, although Natalie does not realize it until many days later, Kilgannon is by no means totally docile, or stupid. Even in this scene, after he has picked her up in his arms he startles her by proving smart enough not to release her until she dutifully says, "Simon says." So, too, she is not yet fully aware that to assume a dominant role in a relationship is nonetheless to commit oneself to a relationship. This is distinctly different from keeping one's individuality totally free.

Then the "game" aspect of the evening is shattered. Looking at the top of Kilgannon's head, Natalie sees a metal plate.

Unfortunately, this perfectly set-up moment, a moment pivotal to the whole movie, is badly undercut by Coppola's decision to opt for fancy camera work (something he has rarely indulged in). The audience should be hit as hard as Natalie is by suddenly seeing Kilgannon's metal plate. But Coppola does not show us the metal plate. He does not even directly show us Natalie's face as she reacts to the sight of the metal plate. Instead, he offers the audience a mirror-reflection of part of Natalie's face as she looks down and sees the plate. In doing so, Coppola lost eighty per cent of the potential impact contained in this dramatic moment.

Despite this blunder, the sequence establishes the film's one outstanding strength: its presentation of character. The developing relationship between Natalie and Kilgannon more than compensates for the vagueness concerning Natalie's marriage. Natalie's present actions, thoughts, and feelings become so interesting we gradually abandon our desire to know more about her past.

The uneven quality of the film is documented in the next sequence, one of the worst Coppola ever directed. It is poor both in form and in content. The camera work is almost amateurish. At least some of the time only one stationary camera was used. As a result, the many actors have to crowd within a very narrow area even when they are supposed to be physically active. The acting, on the whole, is also amateurish—awkward, self-conscious, mechanical. In defense of the actors it must be said that the lines and the situations they are asked to bring to life are much too contrived.

The sequence features Ellen, Kilgannon's former girl friend, and her family. Kilgannon greets Ellen's father at the drive-in the father manages. The father barely remembers who Kilgannon is, yet he immediately invites Kilgannon and Natalie home with him—without even phoning ahead first. Although Natalie now wants to get away from Kilgannon, she accepts the father's invitation (because, of course, it is essential to Coppola's plot that she stick around). At the house, Ellen is instantly nasty to Kilgannon. Neither parent makes any attempt to find out privately how Ellen feels about her former boy friend. Ellen's father first, without any hesitation, offers Kilgannon a full-time job and then completely reneges. The whole sequence is an obvious and lame contrivance created to bring Kilgannon and Natalie still closer together.

After Natalie and Kilgannon leave the house, another weakness in the movie becomes evident. Because Coppola was ad-libbing so much of the script, there is a woeful lack of successful transitions in the movie. Natalie and Kilgannon are at Ellen's home in West Virginia in one scene. In the next, they are in Tennessee—because Coppola decided to use a parade as his next dramatic backdrop. (He ended up presenting far too many shots of the parade itself, slowing down the film's pace still more.)

The lack of transitions led Coppola to pretend that absolutely nothing of any consequence occurs during the sudden leaps in time and geography. The audience is expected to believe that nothing affecting the relationship between Natalie and Kilgannon was said or done during all the hours they rode together, ate together, and, perhaps, slept together between the time they drove from West Virginia to Tennessee—or, later, drove from Tennessee to Nebraska. The same problem with transitions occurs concerning Natalie and Gordon. At the end of a long evening out together on a date not shown on the screen, Gordon brings Natalie to his trailer where Gordon's daughter greets them. Natalie—and the movie audience—is quite startled; apparently, despite all the time they spent together, and despite Gordon's intention to bring Natalie to his home, he never mentioned that he had a daughter living with him.

However, the film's foremost virtue, its development of realistic and interesting characters, begins to reassert itself in the Tennessee sequence. Natalie phones her husband a second time and tells him she realizes now that she is to blame for her problems. She stresses again that she does not want any responsibilities. Acting on this resolution, she abandons Kilgannon—then changes her mind and returns for him, finding him at a bus depot. At that moment, despite what she has just told her husband, she has accepted—at least for the present—a new responsibility. Significantly, she now tells Kilgannon her real name.

Natalie's about-face is completely believable—and this is all to the credit of Coppola and his two leading actors. The very intensity with which Natalie shouts over the phone that she wants to be free is a tip-off that she is being pulled in the opposite direction. She is really shouting at Kilgannon more than at her husband. She is, most of all, shouting at herself. Her contradictory behavior is rendered believable even more by the skillful acting of Knight and Caan. With great subtlety they convey the mounting affection they feel for each other.

By the time the couple reaches Mr. Alfred's zoo in Nebraska, Natalie is riding an emotional rollercoaster. Her love for Kilgannon is growing. And, for this very reason, she is all the more keen on separating herself from him. Never a fool, she perceives that Alfred agrees to hire Kilgannon because he intends to exploit Kilgannon's brawn just as he has exploited the animals he has imprisoned. Though very upset, Natalie flees the scene.

Irony once more enters her life. Precisely because she so much wants to leave Kilgannon behind her, she speeds away—and is stopped from leaving him by a highway policeman, Gordon, who proceeds to give her a speeding ticket and to complicate her life still further.

At first, she is, again, beguiled by sexual possibilities. She realizes that Gordon (played by Robert Duvall) is sexually attracted to her. It appears she is now going to gain the no-strings-attached sexual relationship she originally wanted with Kilgannon. Gordon, though, has already written out the ticket; and, in order to pay the fine, Natalie must return to Alfred's place, for he is the justice of the peace.

Despite this contrivance, the next scenes are dramatically strong. Complications multiply—complications not due to more contrived coincidences, but to the lifelike turns and twists of the characters. Back at the zoo, Natalie discovers an enraged Alfred. He, who thought (as Natalie once did) that he was going to manipulate Kilgannon easily, has been defeated, at least temporarily, by his employee. Kilgannon has freed most of the animals. What was subtly hinted at during the "Simon Says" game, and by Kilgannon's tightening hold on Natalie, is now made more obvious. Mentally "slow" though he is, Kilgannon has a strong will of his own. Even as Natalie pleads with him to stop freeing the animals, he continues to do so. The situation is only resolved by the shrewd Alfred. He drops the charges against Kilgannon in return for $800 of the $1,000 Kilgannon had.

If *The Rain People* were a silly sentimental love story, at this point Natalie and Kilgannon would embrace, and she, panting slightly, would tell him she will "somehow" work things out for them. But Natalie does no such thing. Kilgannon declares his love for her; and she, hesitantly, confesses her fondness for him. But she is also thoroughly exasperated with him.

Complications are not resolved; instead, they continue to multiply. She phones her husband again. Just as Kilgannon is coming to dominate her journey westward, her husband dominates the phone conversation—in order, paradoxically, to tell her that he will obey her wishes. If she wants to get an abortion, he will help her do so. He will do anything she wants.

But Vinny's increased passivity is contrasted by Kilgannon's increased aggressiveness. Jealous of her husband and hungry for her attention, Kilgannon rips out the telephone wires. Badgered and confused by the complications that have come as the result of her flight from all complications, Natalie is furious. She smacks Kilgannon across the face. Driving off, she makes it clear that this time she has no intention of coming back for him.

It is a shame that the last sequence in the film is weak. If Coppola had created a climax of first-rate quality, *The Rain People* could have been, all in all, a success. But the flaws in this final sequence greatly dilute its power.

The climax is flawed not only, as Coppola himself pointed out, because it fails to confront and resolve the thematic core of the script. It is flawed also in terms of plot and characters. That Gordon had made no arrangements to get his daughter Rosalie out of the way so that he could bed down Natalie is hard to believe. That Natalie would, at the very last minute, suddenly decide not to have sex with Gordon is equally implausible (though Coppola tries to

make it acceptable by having Natalie somehow intuit that Gordon is
pretending Natalie is his now-dead wife, and then having her reject
him for this reason). Most implausible of all is the sudden reappear-
ance of Kilgannon. We are expected to believe that, in a relatively
short time, the "slow" Kilgannon was able to investigate and learn
all about the man Natalie was going to go out with, including where
Gordon lived, and make his way to the trailer camp because he
somehow also knew that Natalie would turn up there about the time
that he did.

Still, the climax does have its strong points. For instance, in a
movie focusing on responsibility, the presence of Rosalie is dramatically incisive. Gordon, whom Natalie assumes is a free-wheeling
spirit, has in fact serious responsibilities. Natalie is pressured by the
baby in her womb and the "baby" she picked up along the highway;
and Gordon is equally pressured by *his* offspring, Rosalie.

A further irony is that Rosalie very much wants to be considered
an adult, indicated by her desire to wear a brassiere and to be given
special adult privileges. Rosalie is also well aware of the complexities of human experience. Wandering through the trailer camp
with Kilgannon, she comments on the mixed-up lives of the people
in the other trailers. She sums the matter up by commenting, "It's
complicated." While Natalie fights off being a mother, Rosalie wants
to stop being a child.

During the scene in which Gordon and Natalie are in bed together, Gordon's insistence that he and his now-dead wife shared no
genuine love is juxtaposed with flashbacks that make it clear Gordon
passionately loved his wife. Natalie does not know how to cope with
her marriage, with her pregnancy, and with Kilgannon. Gordon
does not know how to cope with the loss of his wife. Both are trying
to run away from reality through sex. Both fail miserably to get what
they want.

When Gordon ardently pursues sexual conquest, Natalie pulls
back. She grabs Gordon's gun in order to hold him off. At this
moment, she does something even more significant than confessing
her real name to Kilgannon at the bus depot. She tells Gordon that
she is pregnant. Her immediate purpose is to try to coax Gordon
into letting her alone. But the confession could also be a sign that
she is finally ready to accept her pregnancy and her adult responsibilities.

Natalie needs to say more here. Unfortunately, perhaps because he did not know what to have Natalie say, Coppola cuts off this potentially rich opportunity to push his thematic material to some sort of conclusion. Worse, in the next moments he avoids resolving in any way the basic situation of the film—the relationship between Natalie and Kilgannon. After having so badly contrived to put Kilgannon back into the plot, all Coppola does with his character is to kill him off.

Kilgannon, followed by Rosalie, bursts into the trailer. He is ready to protect his "parent." So is Rosalie ready to protect hers. She shoots and kills Kilgannon.

Many of the critics, though cracking down hard on some other aspects of the film, quite rightly praised the actors' performances. It is true that Shirley Knight could have concentrated less on Natalie's neurotic tendencies and more on her motherliness. But other than that, she did a fine job. She vividly conveyed the tension in Natalie, her coldness, her confusion, and her increasingly desperate attempts to escape the complications in her life. Robert Duvall, working with much less material, cleverly managed to indicate that Gordon was not the confident "free spirit" he at first pretended to be. James Caan made a very difficult role appear easy as pie to do. Badly portrayed, Kilgannon could have seemed a character slyly pretending to be mentally slow—which would have made a mess of the movie. Or he could have been reduced to a simpleton (such as Lennie in *Of Mice and Men*)—which would also have ruined the movie. Caan was able to avoid both extremes and, in so doing, render the relationship between Natalie and Kilgannon plausible, and fascinating.

If it is fair to blame Coppola to some extent for the poor performances turned in by members of the *Finian's Rainbow* cast, he should also receive some of the credit for the fine performances by Knight, Caan, and Duvall. Despite his troubles with Knight, he must have been doing something right on the set. His work with Caan in particular should be singled out for praise. In the years right after *The Rain People* was filmed, Caan played a variety of interesting roles (including the role of Sonny Corleone in *The Godfather*). But he never equalled the quality of his effort in *The Rain People* under Coppola's direction.

In other ways, however, Coppola must be faulted for his work on *The Rain People*. His film was not a box-office success, and it did not deserve to be. It is too slow-moving. The photography, for several reasons, is poor. The acting in some of the minor roles is amateurish. The script is contrived, sloppy, and inconclusive.

Yet the film is well worth seeing. For, through its characters and best scenes, it makes a powerful statement about the human experience—its complexities and the responsibilities it entails. Many, many pictures have focused on people who "take to the open road." But very few of these films are as honest as *The Rain People.* Very few of them make it clear, as Coppola's film does, that there is no such thing as "the open road," that people take their problems, their immaturity, their prevarications, their vain desires, and their shallow beliefs right along with them—and meet, wherever they go, other people with the same limitations.

Some of the characters in *The Rain People* are escapists. They do not want serious responsibilities. But the film itself is not an escapist film. It states that no one can escape from himself or his responsibilities.

In offering a realistic delineation of the human being—warts and all—Coppola employs a device he will use again, though not as subtly, in *The Conversation* and *The Godfather, Part II*—irony. Several times, the actions of the characters, actions motivated by a particular desire, lead to consequences antipodal to that desire. The characters are not helped, but bedeviled by what they do. Irony, then, reenforces the realistic portrait of man by underscoring man's limitations.

Coppola did something else—something quite unusual—that makes his film well worth seeing. He filled the screen with interesting ordinary people. Natalie and Kilgannon, and Gordon and Alfred, are not stereotypes. Nor are they—like the characters in *You're A Big Boy Now*—stereotypes given a few individual "twists." For this reason they cannot easily be compared with numerous other film characters. They are unique.

This is quite an achievement. Yet, curiously enough, it is an achievement that causes the viewer to be impatient with *The Rain People* in a way he is almost never impatient with other films. Because Natalie and Kilgannon are not types, the viewer does not think he knows all about them the moment he sees them on the screen. He wants to learn more about them and feels frustrated when that information is not presented to him.

The Rain People is not a success. But, at its best, it is more rewarding than many successful films.

5

"They Think I'm Living This Golden Life"

BECAUSE OF THE LENGTH of time involved before a major film is released to the public, Coppola finished work on *The Rain People* before *Finian's Rainbow* opened at movie houses across the nation. He was exhausted by the weeks of intense work on *The Rain People*. He had become still more apprehensive about the reception his $3,500,000 musical would receive. On top of all this, he now began to worry about how the critics and the general public would react to his newest "personal" film.

When Joseph Gelmis interviewed Coppola, the tense young director tended to ramble. He said, "*The Rain People* could be an awful picture . . . . It doesn't protect itself at all. It's not even sensational. No sex. Very sincere. And I don't even know how terrific it is . . . . I'm tired."

At another point, in an explosion of nerves, Coppola declared, "It's come to the point where I just want to get out altogether. I just want to go do my own thing. And I may do that. I'm fed up. It takes too much out of you." He went on, "I think a lot of people are jealous of me. Basically, my contemporaries. They say, 'Well, there he is, twenty-eight, twenty-nine years old, he's got a lot of money and he's making movies.' They wouldn't want it. Not much. They want it. They just think I'm living this golden life and they don't realize that I am really straining and endeavoring to find some honest balance with myself in terms of the work of the future."

Coppola talked economics. "If I would accept two or three of the forty films I've been offered, I could make a million . . . . I could make a lot of money by just grabbing up three pictures and having writers write them and having cutters cut them, and just—zoom— go right through them. I could pile up about a million dollars, which I would surely like. Because I have no money now whatsoever. I

Marlon Brando (Don Vito Corleone) in The Godfather
Credit: The Museum of Modern Art/Film Stills Archive

spent it all. I lived on what I made on *Finian*. How do you think I made *Rain People?*"

He reemphasized, "All I know is that I'm tired. It's not just opening-night jitters. I've been thinking about this now for six months. I'm tired."

When Gelmis mentioned that Coppola had successfully carried out his Hitler-strategy of joining and working within the Establishment, Coppola replied, "That's what I did. Here I am. But now I don't know if I'm totally satisfied with where it's all led me."[1]

American Zoetrope

Unlike many harrassed Hollywood artists, when Coppola had rested up and regained control of his nerves, he did not quietly rejoin the Establishment ranks. Instead, he pursued a project given further impetus by the mood he was in while talking with Gelmis. The project was American Zoetrope, a production center for young filmmakers, its name borrowed from a toy that was one of the most entertaining of the early nineteenth-century forerunners of the motion picture.

Although many of his peers, at graduate school and elsewhere, had branded him a "sell-out," although Coppola himself had baldly stated he was going to compromise and work within the Establishment in order to achieve his own ends (a philosophy that many people used in order to rationalize their total capitulation to the Establishment), Coppola did have a genuine desire to help other, younger people who wanted to make movies. As president of American Zoetrope, he planned to increase his own directorial power; but, at the same time, he would offer younger directors the opportunities they very much wanted. Coppola was both a pragmatist and an idealist.

"Established Hollywood directors," he stated, "don't do very much to help new talent break into directing. The problem here is that unique Hollywood principle: 'I want my film to be good and his to be lousy.' " He added, "It's different in Europe. European directors who gain some degree of power and influence use their position to sponsor talent they find promising. Men like Tony Richardson and François Truffaut have helped new directors get their start . . . . Not all Hollywood directors have the amount of leverage this sort of thing requires, but enough of them have a strong enough position to be able to extend some help if they really wanted to."[2]

Such sweeping generalizations might not bear up under close scrutiny. Nonetheless, moving beyond rhetoric, Coppola did provide just that kind of help via American Zoetrope. He especially wanted to help young directors coming out of film schools. He worked, for example, with Steve White of UCLA, Robert Dalva of the University of Southern California, and, particularly, George Lucas, the young man who had assisted Coppola on *The Rain People*.

Coppola established American Zoetrope in San Francisco, in a warehouse on Folsom Street. He purchased the equipment and set up the facilities necessary for doing editing, mixing, and sound recording. Warner Brothers, still very optimistic about the box-office potential of the newly released *Finian's Rainbow* and the forthcoming *The Rain People*, funded almost all of the project. Coppola explained that Warner Brothers "wanted to sponsor the programme and saw me as the ideal intermediary between so-called 'established film activity' and the young film-makers that they were then so anxious to become involved with."[3] Young directors would make films, and Warner Brothers would finance and distribute them.

At first, the project gained the attention of many people interested in movies, professionals as well as beginners. Stanley Kubrick and Coppola "exchanged weekly letters on post-*2001: A Space Odyssey* techniques, John Schlesinger expressed interest, Mike Nichols asked how he could invest in American Zoetrope, Haskell Wexler planned to base his new company on Folsom Street, John Korty leased a set of offices, and even Orson Welles was going to do a film with Zoetrope."[4]

The first major full-length film that American Zoetrope completed was *THX-1138*. This science-fiction film about a drugged, loveless society, enslaved by its own technology, was an expanded version of a fifteen-minute film George Lucas had made while still a student. When representatives from Warner Brothers saw the full-length version, they did not like it at all.

An even more ominous development was the financial failure of, first, *Finian's Rainbow* and, later, *The Rain People*.

Other troubles mounted. "My enthusiasm and my imagination,"

Coppola later remarked, "far outpaced any kind of financial logic." Coppola cited other problems. He realized that "there was no cohesive philosophical idea which held the various people together. The only principle we had was young film-makers and freedom, and it was very vague." A final problem "was that lots of people really abused the place and used it for their own purposes without in any way enriching it. Thousands of people wrote and came and sent their films. At first, to avoid being like a Hollywood studio, we tried to see them. At one point there were three people whose only jobs were reading these letters and talking with these people. I kept that up for seven months."

More and more people were admitted into the Folsom Street set-up. Some of them "would use or borrow or steal our equipment. The first year of operation we lost almost $40,000 worth of equipment. Other stuff was damaged, and company cars were taken and cracked up. It was tremendously irresponsible."[5]

Approximately six months after the project began operations, Warner Brothers soured on this "youth movement." *THX-1138*, as feared, also proved to be a financial failure. Warner Brothers pulled out.

Coppola attempted to turn the fortunes of the project around. Commercials for television were made to try to help pay some of the mounting bills. An educational film service and an advertising department were set up for the same purpose. However, nothing could make the project financially profitable. And Coppola was again in debt.

The *Patton* Script

American Zoetrope's severe financial difficulties, breeding Coppola's money woes, serve as a reminder of the precariousness of a Hollywood artist's career. Though still a young man, Coppola had already seen his reputation soar and plummet more than once. Furthermore, because of the peculiar profession he was in, his reputation soared and plummeted not only in relation to assignments just completed, but also according to work done a year—or more—earlier.

Time lags had all sorts of effects. A severe delay between the time Coppola envisioned how he wanted to film *You're A Big Boy Now* and the time when the movie was released made it appear much less fresh in ideas, for critics had already seen several other pictures done in the same style. The delay in time before *Finian's Rainbow* was released and reviewed allowed Coppola to reap the benefits of the temporary high esteem in which Warner Brothers held him. When *Finian's Rainbow* and *The Rain People* flopped, his career quickly suffered.

But the past was still not through with him. For it was just at this time that *Patton,* with Coppola and Edmund H. North credited for the film-script, reached the public.

Patton immediately became a box-office winner. It was one of the biggest financial and critical successes of 1970. George C. Scott won an Oscar for his excellent performance in the title role. And Coppola and North won Academy Awards for their contribution to the movie. Although Coppola's reputation was not altered as dramatically as it had been in earlier years, his stock certainly, again, rose in value.

Actually, there were several scripts written for *Patton,* including scripts preceding Coppola's. Producer Frank McCarthy "had struggled through endless writers and drafts to get the story of George S. Patton off the ground."[6] He hired Coppola to do a script in 1964. Coppola—whose military experience was limited to a short stay in a military school—diligently researched the life of the famous World War Two American general.

His reaction was emphatic. "I said, 'Wait a minute, this guy was obviously nuts. If they want to make a film glorifying him as a great American hero, it will be laughed at. And if I write a film that condemns him, it won't be made at all.' "

Coppola's solution to the problem proved to be a major step toward the ultimately successful presentation of Patton's life on the screen. He decided to make Patton "a man out of his time, a pathetic hero, a Don Quixote figure." In this way, the film would be able to feature two approaches simultaneously. "The people who wanted to see him as a bad guy could say, 'He was crazy, he loved war.' The people who wanted to see him as a hero could say, 'We need a man like that now.' And that's exactly the effect the movie had, which is why it was so successful."

Perhaps the single most famous scene in the movie is the opening scene. Coppola later described its origin. "I was playing with a presentational style—the idea that you have a character just stand in front of the audience for five minutes, and the audience would know more about him just by looking at him than if you went into his past and told about his family life. That's why the best part of that film, in my opinion, is the opening scene. It was the best scene in my script too."[7]

Of course a critic is on just as shaky ground when he praises a writer for a film that other writers worked on as he is when he castigates a writer for a film other writers worked on. The reason that one can, with some degree of confidence, praise Coppola at least in general terms for his work on *Patton* is that Coppola's script was singled out by George C. Scott, who had much to say about the filming of the story.

According to Coppola, he "worked six months on that script . . . . It was a pretty definitive script. But there was a big time lag, and I never had anything to do with it again. They had rewritten my script many times and thrown it out and got different writers." When the part was offered to Scott, "he remembered my script and told them that he would do it if they could use the old script. Scott is the one who resurrected my version."[8]

In his later version of the script, however, Edmund H. North made significant changes.

The story begins in 1943. When German Field Marshal Rommel delivers a crushing defeat to the American forces in North Africa, General Patton is brought in to take command of the American tank units. Patton, confident and flamboyant, greatly improves the morale of the men now under his leadership. In one of the most spectacular battle scenes ever filmed Patton steers his men to a decisive victory over the Germans. The enemy is soon compelled to withdraw from North Africa.

Patton is next assigned to duty in Sicily. He is supposed to provide support for British Field Marshal Montgomery, whom Patton sees only as a rival. Patton disobeys orders and, on his own, captures Messina, the Allied forces' main target. He gets into still more trouble when he visits a field hospital. There he slaps the face of a soldier suffering from battle fatigue.

The incident receives much publicity. Commander Dwight D. Eisenhower insists that Patton apologize in front of the troops. Patton is also relieved of his command. However, he returns to active service in northern Europe, leads his men through an impasse at Normandy and also, later, moving at great speed, rescues another part of the army. He continues to prove a successful, if prickly, commander right through to the end of the war.

Then, ever the individualist, he runs into still more trouble. He refuses to suppress his hatred for the Russians. He insults them at diplomatic functions and makes other remarks that are publicized. Once more, he is relieved of his command.

To the degree that *Patton* dramatizes the actions of a man of action, the film is a first-rate example of one traditional kind of motion picture. The North African tank battle is surely the finest battle featuring mechanized weaponry ever put on the screen. But *Patton* at its most interesting does not operate within a popular traditional framework. From the very start, its *major* emphasis is on a man's character rather than on his actions as a soldier. Some day a finer tank battle than the one in *Patton* may be staged, but the outstanding presentation of the character General Patton is unique and will never be superseded.

The majority of critics centered their attention on the character delineation of Patton. Stanely Kauffmann wrote that "McCarthy and Schaffner [the director] had either prescience or blind luck . . . . They commissioned a screenplay by Francis Ford Coppola and Edmund H. North that emphasizes the contradictions of their hero."[9] Rex Reed listed a few of Patton's traits. Patton "was religious yet profane, brutal yet easily moved to tears. He was so flamboyant and theatrical that he even went so far as to design the uniforms of his tank crewmen . . . . He firmly believed he was reincarnated." Reed summed up this character-sketch by stating, "Fortunately, the script for *Patton* is so well-researched and brilliantly thought out that it examines both the faults and the virtues of the man without leaning too heavily in either direction."[10]

Other critics believed that the examination of Patton did gradually lean heavily in one direction. Vincent Canby remarked, "The movie . . . is a huge, initially ambivalent but finally adoring, Pop portrait of one of the most brilliant and outrageous American military figures of the last 100 years."[11] Joseph Morgenstern elaborated on this position. He stated that the film, "though seductive and constantly entertaining, is the muddled glorification of a madman." Later, he added, "Time and again Patton is portrayed as a deceitful, self-justifying megalomaniac who can't follow orders. Yet the movie makes shrewd, sentimental capital of the soldier-slapping incident and Patton's subsequent fall from favor . . . . The closer Patton comes to lunacy, the more the movie encourages us to laugh at him as a lovable, irascible old coot who can't understand politics and can't keep his tactless mouth shut."[12]

The film does drift toward an ever-more-sympathetic, affirmative view of Patton. It is hard to conceive of its becoming a big box-office success if it did not do so. This gradual tipping of the scales, however, is never so blatant and insistent as to offend the members of the audience who would find a romanticized depiction of war and the warrior intolerable. Furthermore, the film very much appealed to those viewers (and there may have been many such viewers) who were neither one hundred per cent for war nor one hundred per cent against war, but who had ambivalent feelings about war and about this kind of national hero.

What is finally most important is that the portrait of Patton does contain so much ambiguity—so many richly realistic contradictions. No matter who—Coppola or North—contributed precisely which brushstrokes to the portrait, the end result (capped by Scott's superb performance) is the presentation of one of the most complex and fascinating characters shown on the screen. At its frequent best, the presentation does make it difficult to label this character. For he will not simplify himself in order to make it easy for someone to judge him. He won't "hold still."

The film, indeed, excitingly dramatizes the fact that whether a person is good or bad, praiseworthy or a fool, often depends on the specific situation within which he is operating. Leading American soldiers in an attack (particularly in the North African campaign), for instance, Patton achieved outstanding success. He was invaluable. When this same person was placed in a situation demanding diplomacy, he was comically inept or, worse, a dangerous liability.

To complicate matters still more (and, so, to make matters even more lifelike), Patton is shown to be a "good guy" and a "bad guy" simultaneously. From the poverty-stricken peasant's point of view, Patton was certainly wrong in shooting the peasant's animal because it impeded the forward thrust of Allied tanks. The American tankmen, on the other hand, believed Patton was dead right. Patton was wrong to disobey orders; an army cannot function under such conditions. Yet he was right to disobey; he led the troops to victory, which is, after all, the ultimate goal.

Frequently, if a person's actions do not make it easy to evaluate him, a shift of focus from actions to motivations simplifies the problem nicely. But the script for *Patton* is so realistic, such a shift cannot smoothly resolve the problem. The film makes it clear that Patton was spurred to action by multiple motivations. He revered and tried to embody admirable ancient ideals, and he vaingloriously lusted after fame. He strove to utilize his intellect and create strategy that would outwit the enemy commander, and he had a raw desire to destroy. He wanted to test his courage, and he simply loved war.

Finally, if one decides one cannot judge Patton at all because he was insane, one must then agree that not all madmen should be locked up—at least not all of the time. For sometimes madmen prove very useful to society. And what, in turn, does this reveal about society?

The Coppola-North script was undoubtedly greatly enhanced by the skill of George C. Scott. But the script itself is praiseworthy. Coppola's career-long preoccupation, as a writer and a director, with an emphasis on character rather than plot thrived on the material provided for him in *Patton*.

6

"I Decided It Could Be A *Good* Movie"

IN AN ARTICLE reprinted in *The Godfather Papers*, Mario Puzo described in detail how he came to write his most famous novel. His first novel, *The Dark Arena*, was published in 1955. Ten years later *The Fortunate Pilgrim*, his second novel, appeared. The two books brought Puzo $6,500. When he asked his publisher, Atheneum, to give him an advance so that he could start work on a third novel, his request was turned down.

Startled, Puzo talked with the editors at Atheneum and was told that they did not like the basic concept of the new novel he had in mind. At this moment one of the editors remarked that he wished that Puzo had further developed a minor character in *The Fortunate Pilgrim* who worked for the Mafia. Puzo later commented, "I was forty-five years old and tired of being an artist. Besides, I owed $20,000 to relatives, finance companies, banks and assorted bookmakers and shylocks. It was really time to grow up and sell out as Lenny Bruce once advised."

He agreed to write a novel centered on the Mafia. He wrote a ten-page outline of the novel. Atheneum rejected the project. And that was the end of the literary-business relationship between Atheneum and Puzo.

Months went by, months in which Puzo did various kinds of free-lance writing. One day he had lunch with an old friend. "During lunch," Puzo recalled, "I told him some funny Mafia stories and my ten-page outline. He was enthusiastic. He arranged a meeting for me with the editors of G. P. Putnam's Sons. The editors just sat around for an hour listening to my Mafia tales and said go ahead. They also gave me a $5,000 advance."

Despite working on other literary projects concurrently, Puzo wrote *The Godfather* in three years. Although he wrote the novel strictly from research material and had no direct connections with

95

any gangsters, after the book appeared Puzo heard a story about himself that quite pleased him: "I heard . . . that the Mafia had paid me a million dollars to write *The Godfather* as a public relations con . . . . I treasure the compliment."

There were more gratifying moments to come. When Puzo learned that the paperback rights to the new novel were going to be sold for over $400,000, he began phoning his brothers and sisters. "The reason for this was because every Italian family has a 'chooch,' a donkey. That is, a family idiot everybody agrees will never be able to make a living and so has to be helped without rancor or reproach. I was the family 'chooch' and I just wanted to tell them I was abdicating the family role."

Having sold the movie rights to the book before it became a best seller, Puzo had no interest in a film version of his book—until he read in the newspapers one day that Danny Thomas wanted to play the title role in the film version. Puzo panicked.

As was soon to be the case with Coppola, Puzo envisioned Marlon Brando in the title role. Puzo even acted on his idea. "Through a mutual friend, Jeff Brown, I contacted Brando, wrote him a letter, and he was nice enough to call me. We had a talk on the phone. He had not read the book but he told me that the studio would never hire him unless a strong director insisted on it."

What Puzo did not know was that, despite what Danny Thomas and other actors thought the situation was, Paramount at that time did not plan to make a movie of *The Godfather*. Recently another picture made by Paramount about the Mafia, *The Brotherhood,* had been released and proved a financial failure. Paramount changed its mind about filming Puzo's book only when the novel proceeded to become a best seller.

Then, Puzo recounted, "Al Ruddy, the producer, was assigned to the film, and he came to New York, saw my agent and said Paramount wanted me to do the script. It would be a low budget, he said, so they couldn't offer to pay me much. I turned the offer down. They found more money and a percentage and I agreed to see Al Ruddy."

Ruddy had produced the highly successful *Hogan's Heroes* television series and the movie *Little Fauss and Big Halsey,* a box-office disappointment. Not long after Puzo and Ruddy met, Puzo was in Hollywood, writing the first draft of the screenplay. Puzo told the studio about his desire to have Brando in the picture—and received a cold response. While Puzo was rewriting his script, Coppola was hired. According to Puzo, it was Peter Bart "who came up with the idea of using Francis Coppola as the director. Mainly because he was Italian and young." Puzo could not help wondering "if they picked Coppola because he was a kid in his early thirties and had just directed two financial failures, and so could be controlled." One of the main concerns of the studio, and why it wanted to exert as much control over the filming of *The Godfather* as possible, was its strong desire to keep the cost of the film down as near to one million dollars as possible. The film ultimately cost over five million dollars.

Ruddy talked again with Puzo. " 'The one thing Francis and I want you to understand,' Ruddy told me, 'is that there is no intention of his rewriting your script. Francis just wants to direct and everybody is happy with your work.' I knew *immediately* that I had a writing partner."

Although Puzo's instincts were not always correct, they were right this time. Coppola, Puzo related, "rewrote one half and I rewrote the second half. Then we traded and rewrote each other. I suggested we work together. Francis looked me right in the eye and said no. That's when I knew he was really a director." Nonetheless, Puzo and Coppola got along well. Puzo later stressed that Coppola "earned his half of the screen credit."

The Puzo-Coppola partnership worked out well in regard to another important matter. Both of them wanted Brando in the picture, despite the continued opposition to the idea by the studio heads. "Francis Coppola," Puzo said, "is heavy-set, jolly, and is usually happy-go-lucky. What I didn't know was that he could be tough about his work. Anyway he fought and got Brando."

Puzo witnessed what went on during casting tryouts. "Actors would come in and talk to Coppola and exert all their art and skills to make him remember them. I sat in on some interviews. Coppola was cool and courteous to these people, but for me it was simply too painful. I quit. I couldn't watch them anymore. They were so vulnerable, so open, so naked in their hope for lightning to strike."[1]

Coppola later described the conflicts involved in casting decisions, especially concerning Brando. He also detailed how, at the invitation of Paramount's Peter Bart, he became a part of the making of *The Godfather*. "When I was offered the project, I started to read the book and I got only about 50 pages into it. I thought it was a popular, sensational novel, pretty cheap stuff." He turned down the offer.

"Four or five months later . . . I was in dire financial straits."[2]

Zoetrope operations had put him $300,000 in debt. Bart again phoned and offered him the job of directing *The Godfather*.

What happened next has been told many times.

Coppola put his hand over the receiver and turned to his friend George Lucas. He said, "George, what should I do? Should I make this gangster picture or shouldn't I?"

"Francis," Lucas replied, "we need the money."

Coppola told Bart, "Okay, I'm in."

If Coppola was still not sure he wanted to proceed, he soon became firmly committed to the project. What removed all uncertainty was a thorough reading of Puzo's novel. He said later, "I got into what the book is really about—the story of the family, this father and his sons, and questions of power and succession—and I thought it was a terrific story, if you cut out all the other stuff. I decided it could be not only a successful movie but also a *good* movie."

Coppola also said that if both *Godfather* pictures "are strong, it's because of what Mario originally put in his book that was strong and valid . . . . I have great respect for Mario. He created the story, he created the characters, even in *Part II*, which I wrote more of than *Part I*. But all the key elements go back to his book."

Asked why he thought Paramount approached him about directing the film, Coppola replied, "The book hadn't yet made an impression. A lot of directors, including Richard Brooks and Costa-Gavras, had already turned it down. At that time, I had an interesting reputation as a director who could make a film economically."

Coppola's desire to cast Brando evolved over a period of time. "I must have interviewed 2000 people. We video-taped every old Italian actor in existence. But it became apparent that the role called for an actor of such magnetism, such charisma, just walking into a room had to be an event. We concluded that if an Italian actor had gotten to be 70 years old without becoming famous on his own, he wouldn't have the air of authority we needed."

After discussing the problem with the studio heads, Coppola and they "finally figured that what we had to do was hire the best *actor* in the world. It was that simple. It boiled down to Laurence Olivier or Marlon Brando, who *are* the greatest actors in the world."

Almost no one at Paramount liked this decision. "Ruddy liked Brando," said Coppola, "but he said flatly that the studio heads would never buy it. We got in touch with [Robert] Evans, pitched Brando and listened to him yell at us for being fools."

Just about this time, Coppola became aware of another development. "By now, the book was becoming more and more successful, and it was outstripping me in terms of my potency as a director. It was getting bigger than I was. And they were starting to wonder if they hadn't made a big mistake in choosing me as the director."

Nevertheless, Coppola stuck to his guns regarding his views on the casting. "Time passed, the book got bigger, the budget increased and I refused to send them any new casting ideas . . . . So a big meeting was scheduled." Presiding at this meeting were Robert Evans and Stanley Jaffe, who was at that time the president of Paramount. Coppola made still another pitch to have Brando in the lead role. "Jaffe replied, and these are his exact words, 'As president of Paramount Pictures, I assure you that Marlon Brando will never appear in this motion picture and, furthermore, as president of the company, I will no longer allow you to discuss it.' "

Coppola insisted that he be allowed to present his case. "Evans persuaded Jaffe to give me five minutes. I stood up as if I were a lawyer pleading for someone's life and went through all the reasons I thought only Brando could play the part."[3] Coppola's main reason was that "the mystique Brando had as an actor amongst other actors would inspire precisely the right kind of awe that the character of Don needed."[4] When he finished talking, Coppola pretended to collapse on the floor.

He was permitted to consider Brando for the role. "He was told he could proceed, on three conditions: that Brando take no salary; that he shoot a screen test; and that he guarantee with his own money that the film would not go over the budget because of his exploits . . . . The feeling at Paramount, shared by industry officials, was that Brando ought to be grateful, since he had a reputation for being difficult and had not had a box-office hit in a decade."[5] (It was later stated that the third condition was dropped. Also, paid a percentage of the profits instead of a salary, Brando did not exactly lose financially.)

Now all Coppola had to do was to maneuver one of the greatest actors in the world into taking a screen test.

As he said later, "You have to realize that . . . I was still scared shitless of Brando. So I called him and said I wanted to explore the role with him. At which point he jumped in and said he wasn't entirely sure he *could* play the role, and if he couldn't, he shouldn't, so why not get together and try it out?"

Coppola thought quickly. "Wonderful," he said, "let's video-tape it."

"Fine," said Brando.

The next day, Coppola, accompanied by a photographer and Salvatore Corsitto, the actor who would play the role of the undertaker, went to Brando's house. Corsitto had memorized the speech in which he asks the Godfather for a favor. "Brando met us in his living room, wearing a Japanees kimono, hair tied back in a ponytail. I just started video-taping him. He began to slide into character. He took some shoe polish and put it in his hair. His speech changed: 'You t'ink I need a mustache?' "

Nervously, Coppola replied, "Oh, yeah, my Uncle Louis has a mustache."

"He dabbed on a phony mustache," Coppola continued, "and, as I video-taped him, he reached for some Kleenex. 'I want to be like bulldog,' he mumbled, and stuffed wads of it into his mouth. He kept talking to himself, mumbling, and finally said, 'I just wanna improvise.' "

Without any explanation, Coppola brought in the "undertaker." He went up to Brando "and launched right into his speech. Brando didn't know what was going on for a moment, but he listened and then just started doing the scene."

The result was a complete success. Coppola "watched 47-year-old Marlon Brando turn into this aging Mafia chief. It was fantastic. Later, when I showed the tape to Evans and Jaffe, their reaction— and this is where I give them credit—was instantaneous. They both said he was great."[6]

Concerning the casting of other roles, Puzo recalled that James Caan and Robert Duvall both tested well. But there was the big question of who should play the role of Michael. "Finally the name of Al Pacino came up . . . . Coppola got hold of a screen test Pacino had done for some Italian movie and showed it. I loved him. I gave Francis a letter saying that above all Pacino had to be in the film."

Inevitably, though, "there were objections. Pacino was too short, too Italian looking. He was supposed to be the American in the family. He had to look a little classy, a little Ivy League. Coppola kept saying a good actor is a good actor."

Pacino tested. "The cameras were running. He didn't know his

lines. He threw in his own words. He didn't understand the character at all. He was terrible."

After the test ended, Puzo went over to Coppola and said, "Give
me my letter back."

"What letter?"

"The one I gave you saying I wanted Pacino."

Coppola shook his head. "Wait a while." In a moment, he said,
"The self-destructive bastard. He didn't even know his lines."

Puzo witnessed Coppola's stubbornness in action. He watched
Coppola and his crew test Pacino all day. "They coached him, they
rehearsed him, they turned him inside out."

A happy ending should have immediately followed. But it did
not. "On screen Pacino still didn't strike *anybody*—excepting
Coppola—as right for the part of Michael. Coppola kept arguing.
Finally Evans said, 'Francis, I must say you're alone in this.' "

"Tests were made of other people," Puzo continued. "There was
even talk of postponing the picture. Coppola kept insisting Pacino
was the right man for the part . . . . But it seemed to be a dead
issue." Then, when Puzo returned from a week's stay in New York,
he learned that "Al Pacino had the part of Michael."

Puzo later mentioned another matter that came to a head before
the picture was released. "The Italian American League began to
make noises. Ruddy asked me if I would sit down with the league to
iron things out. I told him I would not. He decided he would and he
did. He promised them to take out all references to the Mafia in the
script and to preserve the Italian honor. The league pledged its
cooperation in the making of the film . . . . I must say Ruddy proved
himself a shrewd bargainer because the word 'Mafia' was never in
the script in the first place."[7]

Puzo's work on the film came to an end. Coppola pressed on.
Brando was finishing a film in England; Coppola flew over to Cambridge for a week. According to Bob Thomas, "During the day
Coppola wrote *The Godfather* script while Marlon worked in *The
Nightcomers*. At night they discussed Don Corleone and how he
should be played . . . . Marlon, recognizing that Coppola was
scared, was gentle and accommodating; he even brought dinner on
a tray to Coppola's room. The week at Cambridge was helpful for
the director in understanding Marlon. Coppola noted that the
people surrounding Brando were not the usual sycophantic entourage of a movie star. They obviously admired Marlon, but they were

honest with him, too. Coppola decided that was the way Marlon wanted to be treated."

Thomas goes on to say that when the shooting of the film started early in 1971, the pressure began to peak. The first scene Coppola chose to film was the meeting in the Corleones' olive-oil company office. "The scene wasn't working well, and Brando suggested more rehearsal time. Coppola declined; he knew that he was being carefully watched and felt that he had to start shooting. When he saw the footage afterward, he realized his mistake, and asked permission to reshoot the sequence. This seemed to confirm the growing suspicion among Paramount executives that Coppola was too young and inexperienced to handle such an important assignment."[8]

Some of the technicians, including the cinematographer, were surly to Coppola, if not downright insubordinate. Another sore spot was the matter of the budget, which was only gradually raised. Still another problem was the shooting schedule. Coppola said, "I told them it would take me 80 days to make the movie, and they gave me a schedule of 53 days." At one point "Evans started to make inquiries to see if Kazan were available. They figured that Kazan was the only director who could really work with Brando."[9]

Even though Coppola was used to working under pressure, the pressure he felt now was extreme. "If you'd checked with the crew while we were filming," he said, "they'd have said *The Godfather* was going to be the biggest disaster of all time . . . . I couldn't get to sleep at night. When I did, I had nightmares of seeing Elia Kazan walk onto the set, come up to me and say, 'Uh, Francis, I've been asked to . . . .' But Marlon was a great help. When I mentioned the threatening noises, he told me he wouldn't continue the picture if I got fired."[10]

Coppola summed up the first long period of work. "I was getting 'fired' every other week. The things they were going to fire me over were, one: wanting to cast Brando. Two: wanting to cast Pacino. Wanting to shoot in Sicily; wanting to make it in period. The very things that made the film different from any other film."

The turning point came three weeks after the filming started. "I think I only stayed on . . . because literally they made a corporate decision: 'If we don't do it now, we'll delay for six months, and the book's a bestseller now.' I think they decided it would be more trouble to fire me."[11]

Now, knowing he was going to remain as director, Coppola really took charge. He demanded the removal of a few members of the crew. The rest of the crew took notice.

But his problems were still not at an end. One remaining problem was the question of how long the movie should be, and what episodes should be shown in that length of time. "I first felt that I had only two hours. And there were so many obligations that I had. I had to do the Hollywood producer. I hated that whole Hollywood section, but I had to do it because I had to cut off that stupid horse's head. I had to do this, I had to do that. And by the time I did what I had to do, I had already used up the movie. So I never had time to make some of the points I wanted to make."[12]

Despite his lack of genuine interest in the scene, Coppola did a fine job of showing the audience the severed head of the horse. "It was the head of a real, formerly alive horse. We called a dog-food place and bought the head for very little money. The head came packed in dry ice. We did the filming with the ASPCA watching. We gave them the head when we were finished to dispose of it."

Coppola remained irritated by the scene even when it was praised. He could not understand why so many people were so affected by the death of the horse. "What about all the people who died in the movie," he wanted to know.[13]

One scene that Coppola allowed to run much longer than it was scheduled to run was the death of Don Corleone. He told Brando that he did not really know exactly how to shoot that scene and asked Brando how they could make the action involving the grandson believable. Brando said, "Here's how *I* play with kids," Coppola recalled. Then Brando "took an orange peel, cut it into pieces that looked like fangs and slipped them into his mouth . . . . I thought, what a ridiculous idea. Then suddenly I saw it: Of course! The Godfather dies as a monster! And once I'd seen him with the orange-peel fangs, I knew I could never shoot it any other way."[14]

Despite the pressures of time, he allowed the scene to run approximately four minutes. Afterwards, he had no regrets. He came to consider it one of the best scenes in the film.

Coppola realized he no longer had the time to make all of the script revisions still needed. He called in Robert Towne, whom he had met while they both worked for Roger Corman. Towne would win fame for his screenplays *Shampoo* and *Chinatown*. On Coppola's film, Towne made key contributions to the exchanges between Michael and Kay and to the scene in which Michael kills Sollozzo

and McCluskey. Towne wrote almost all of the scene featuring the
Don and Michael discussing the future of the family business.

Yet, although Coppola was relieved of his responsibilities as a
writer, his nerves continued to bother him. Later he recalled, "Al
Ruddy, who's a nice guy but who's more of a wheeler-dealer than I
am, used to walk onto the *Godfather* set now and then to suggest
that an actor wear a hat for such and such a scene. I'd say, 'No, I
already thought this scene out, thanks, anyway.' And no sooner
would the sentence be out of my mouth than I'd think, fuck it, he's
right, the actor *should* be wearing a hat. But I wouldn't, or couldn't,
change it. If it had been George Lucas or someone like that, I'd
have accepted the suggestion. But there are some people you can't
take criticism from, perhaps because you feel threatened."[15]

It is not too surprising, then, that Coppola, although given support by Evans and by Charles Bluhdorn, the head of Gulf & Western, was ready to capitulate to some wishes of the studio bosses. He
was prepared to cut fifteen minutes or more of the film—more than
he himself wanted to cut. Coppola praised Evans for saving those
fifteen minutes of film. "I have to give Bob Evans credit there. As
soon as he saw the film, he decided it would be a major hit. He
staked his career on it, because he was the guy who fought for the
length. I was chicken."

Nonetheless, despite his not making *all* the crucial decisions that
caused *The Godfather* to be one of the all-time box-office successes,
Coppola is the man most responsible for the quality of that film. He
created a good portion of the script. He fought for the casting of
Brando and Pacino. He fought to make the film as a period piece.
And, also as director, he created the totally convincing atmosphere
in the film. "The fact that my background is Italian helped enormously. I made a very conscious decision. I wanted to get all the
Catholic rituals into the film. That's where the idea of the baptism
ending came from. I knew the details. I've almost never seen a
movie that gave any real sense of what it was like to be an Italian-
American."[16]

In the first months of its run the film earned more than one
million dollars in profit each day.

At first, the plot of *The Godfather* centers on Don Vito Corleone,
the head of one of the five Italian-American "families" that operate a
crime syndicate. It is 1945 and the Don's daughter Connie has just
married Carlo Rizzi. Her three brothers, Sonny, Michael, and

Freddie, are at the reception. Michael, who up to this time has not
been involved in his father's activities, has brought his girl friend
Kay Adams to the day's festivities.

But the focus of attention is Don Corleone. Many people come to
see him during the course of the afternoon. Some come merely to
congratulate him on his daughter's marriage or to thank him for his
past help. Some, like the singer Johnny Fontane, seek his help now.
Fontane is getting nowhere with Hollywood producer Jack Woltz,
who is making a film that Fontane very much wants to be in. The
Don sends Tom Hagen, his lawyer and right-hand man, to discuss
the matter with Woltz. Woltz stubbornly refuses to give Fontane
the part—until he wakes up one morning to find the severed head of
his most valuable horse at the foot of his bed.

Not long afterward there is a meeting at which representatives of
other "families" ask Don Corleone to enter the narcotics business
with them. Here, Sonny makes a tactical blunder that ultimately
disrupts the peace among the "families." When the Don rejects the
invitation—because he disapproves of pushing drugs and because
he thinks this activity would spoil the presently smooth relationship
between the "families" and certain powerful politicians, Sonny ex-
presses his disagreement with his father's decision. Sollozzo, a
leader in one of the other "families," believes that if the Don were
dead, Sonny would join the narcotics venture—and decides to have
the Don killed. Although shot five times, in the hospital the Don
fights—successfully—for his life.

It is at this point that Michael is drawn into the world of the
Mafia. While visiting his father in the hospital, Michael senses that
another attempt on his father's life is about to be made. Although
unarmed, he is able to bluff the would-be assassins out of the attempt. Furious that the scheme failed, McCluskey, a police officer
who helped Sollozzo set up the second assassination plot, breaks
Michael's jaw.

Michael helps devise a plan that will allow him to avenge both his
father and himself. His father's men arrange a meeting between
Sollozzo, McCluskey, and Michael. At the restaurant where the
meeting takes place, Michael goes to the men's room, takes a gun
planted there for him, and kills both Sollozzo and McCluskey.

A full-scale gang war erupts. Michael is sent to Sicily for his
safety. There, he marries the beautiful peasant Apollonia. His
enemies, however, learn of his whereabouts and plant a bomb in his

car. But it is Apollonia, not Michael, who is killed by the explosion. While he is in Sicily, his brother-in-law Rizzi betrays Sonny, who is killed.

Aging and weary of the bloodshed, the Don arranges a truce. Afterwards, he permits Michael, now back home and married to Kay, to take over more and more of the Corleones' business activities. The Don retires and soon dies of a heart attack, brought on while he is playing with one of his grandchildren.

The climax of the film begins when Michael arranges for a mass slaying of his enemies, including Rizzi, to occur while he is at the church altar serving as the godfather of his sister's baby. Connie accuses him of being responsible for her husband's death. Kay later asks him if Connie's accusation is true. Michael emphatically denies responsibility. Nonetheless, before he closes the door behind her, she sees the Don's men gathering around Michael to tell him of the successful assassinations and to pay him homage as the new Godfather of the "family."

7

"The Real Godfathers Double-Crossed People"

The Godfather
More Than a Gangster Film

THE INSTANT record-breaking success of *The Godfather* led critics to write about it at great length and led interviewers to discuss it with Coppola, Brando, and others at great length. Excited by its dramatic and financial achievements, many people, including—at times—Coppola himself, made ever greater claims on behalf of the film. Some declared that *The Godfather* was far more than just a gangster film. The film was considered a realistic depiction of the Mafia. Furthermore, the Mafia it portrayed also served, the public was told, as a valid and condemnatory metaphor for the United States.

Such claims do the film no favor.

There is much to admire in *The Godfather*, but the viewer who pays too much attention to such claims will only be distracted from the film's admirable features. Considered carefully, these claims merely reveal some of the film's limitations.

The movie does present its version of a few aspects of Mafia life. But its version is, at best, only partially realistic. The Sicilian sequence, for instance, implies a serious working connection between the Mafia in Sicily and the Mafia in the United States. Actually, the connection has almost always been very tenuous. Lucky Luciano was one of the most powerful American Mafia leaders. When he was deported from the United States, he decided to live in Sicily. The local Mafia leaders there welcomed him with open arms—and soon swindled him out of fifteen million lire.

Nor does the movie offer any factual account of the origin of the Mafia. Puzo's book does take advantage of Michael's presence in Sicily to introduce such information. Although Puzo somewhat

109

James Caan (Sonny Corleone) in The Godfather
Credit: *The Museum of Modern Art/Film Stills Archive*

110 FRANCIS FORD COPPOLA

overemphasized the few features of the original Mafia that made it vaguely similar to a Robin Hood type of organization on occasion, he presented many accurate—that is to say, unattractive—details. Puzo also made it quite clear that the contemporary Sicilian Mafia (and, by implication, the contemporary American Mafia) is extremely repressive. He stated that the Mafia became "a degenerate capitalist structure, anti-communist, anti-liberal, placing its own taxes on every form of business endeavor no matter how small." It developed into "the illegal arm of the rich and even the auxilary police of the legal and political structure."

In the novel, Michael stays in the home of a man who is the uncle of Don Tommasino, a local power in the Mafia. Puzo described Don Tommasino as a man "who for a certain sum of money protected the real estate of the rich from all claims made on it by the poor, legal or illegal. When any poor peasant tried to implement the law which permitted him to buy uncultivated land, [Don Tommasino] frightened him off with threats of bodily harm or death." Puzo added, "Don Tommasino also controlled the water rights in the area and vetoed the local building of any new dams by the Roman government. Such dams would ruin the lucrative business of selling water from the artesian wells he controlled, make water too cheap."[1] None of these unattractive features is emphasized in the movie.

The film avoids other basic truths. Don Corleone embodies absolute loyalty; he is loyal to everyone who is loyal to him. With very rare exception, all of his top men are equally loyal. In reality, the Mafia Dons and their henchmen by no means embodied pure loyalty. They double-crossed each other repeatedly.

In the 1930s, during the gang war between Joe Masseria and Salvatore Maranzano, five of Masseria's top men, including Lucky Luciano and Vito Genovese, decided that Masseria would lose the war. They plotted, successfully, with Maranzano to have Masseria killed. Then Maranzano betrayed those men, double-crossed Thomas Lucchese (one of his own men), and kept the profits that should have gone to several of his underlings. Next, Luciano plotted against Maranzano; he convinced Joe "Bananas" Bonanno and Joseph Profaci, two top men in Maranzano's "army," to betray Maranzano. Learning of the plot, Maranzano planned to have Luciano murdered. But Luciano hired four gunmen to murder Maranzano before the latter could murder him.

Coppola himself has commented on this matter of loyalty. Don

Corleone, Coppola said, "was a synthesis of Genovese and Joseph Profaci, but Genovese ordered his soldiers not to deal in drugs while he himself did just that on the side; Profaci was dishonorable at a lot of levels. The film Godfather would never double-cross anyone, but the real godfathers double-crossed people over and over."[2]

Film critic William S. Pechter commented on the Corleone family's decision not to enter the drug racket. He considered this decision "unlikely"—an attempt "merely to make the Corleones more acceptable to us." There were a few older Mafia figures who were reluctant to deal in heroin, but this was less true in the United States. In any case, the emphasis in Puzo's novel is on the Don's concern for profits and power. He does not consider drug-dealing a dirty business. He is worried only that his political connections might consider it a dirty business. In the movie, one is allowed to believe that the Don himself disapproves of dealing in narcotics. So, too, the movie never makes it clear that the Don was dead wrong in his thinking. Politicians and all kinds of other people readily accepted the increased drug traffic, made money on drugs, and took drugs.

The film does feature the home life of members of the Mafia. Many other gangster films, of course, presented the domestic side of a gangster's life. But, as Pechter stressed, no other film matched the degree of emphasis given in *The Godfather* to this part of a gangster's life. Pechter remarked that we see the men in the Mafia "as members of a 'family': as godfather, father, grandparent, son, and brother. Though we see Don Corleone occasionally issuing an edict on his business affairs, our predominant images of him are not in his exercise of power but in his domestic role—officiating as father of the bride . . . shopping for groceries, playing with his grandchild; not as a Scarface in flashy suits and monogrammed shirts, but as an old man, almost vulnerable-looking in his rumpled clothes and with the trace of gray stubble on his face."[3]

The schemes to kill enemies and to avoid being killed are given added levels of excitement and suspense in the film because of this focus on the Corleones' personal lives. Responding to this new and interesting emphasis on a gangster's domestic life, the audience is more aware that these gangsters are human beings—and, therefore, as vulnerable to a bullet as the rest of us.

Nonetheless, even here the film is not completely realistic. The younger generation of Italians whose fathers or other older male relatives were Mafia members is, as a group, quite different from the young people depicted in *The Godfather*. Consider the biographical information offered in Gay Talese's *Honor Thy Father*.

Joe "Bananas" Bonanno was a top man in the Mafia at approximately the same time the fictitious Vito Corleone was rising to power. Joe Bonanno's son Bill roughly corresponds in time to Michael Corleone. Of course, differences in behavior between Bill Bonanno and Michael Corleone can—in part—be attributed to differences in intelligence and temperament. Still, compared to the fictitious Michael, Talese's portrait of Bill Bonanno is, by far, the more convincing.

Like Michael, Bill only gradually became involved in Mafia activities; he was not "groomed" from birth to be a part of the organization. But there came a time when Bonanno had to make a choice that could mean "giving up . . . the respectable conventional life that most Americans led . . . . He probably did not belong anywhere except at his father's side . . . because, in spite of his education, he was not really qualified to do anything important in the so-called legitimate world. He had not studied hard in school . . . . His attention span had been too short, his ego had perhaps been too large, his father's existence perhaps too distracting for him to progress normally through the educational system."

Later, Talese commented further on this point. Bill "was confident that he could earn a living on his own, although he suspected that in the legitimate world he was at a tremendous disadvantage. With his name . . . he would probably have to start off at the bottom without influential family friends pulling him upward. He would be restricted to menial tasks in an office, which would bore him, or he would work as a traveling salesman."[4]

Yet even more revealing is a comparison of the *women* of Bill Bonanno's generation with the women—and their lovers and husbands—in *The Godfather* films.

When asked why the women in these films were usually so acquiescent, Coppola replied, "That was how the women were represented in the original book and, from what I know, it was the role of women in the Mafia fabric."[5] This was a weak answer. In *The Godfather* Michael courts and marries Kay Adams, who is not an Italian, not a Catholic, but a complete outsider. Bill Bonanno dated women somewhat similar to Kay while he was in high school and college, and later had an affair with a non-Italian woman. But he married an Italian Catholic who was told to be subservient to father and husband.

Bill's wife Rosalie, however, still gave her husband as much trouble as Kay, the outsider, gave Michael—up to the time Kay had the abortion. Other Italian women of that generation who were brought up within the Mafia environment were not only even more rebellious, they were *successfully* rebellious. Bill Bonanno's sister Catherine made a point of marrying a man completely removed from the Mafia world. So did Rosalie's sister Josephine. Josephine "was the first daughter to finish college, and, without being a feminist, she undoubtedly identified with the cause of modern women seeking greater liberation, which was probably one reason, Bill thought, why she disliked him, for he typified everything that she as a modern young woman undoubtedly rejected—he was the dominant Sicilian male who did as he pleased, came and went as he wished, unquestioned, the inheritor of the rights of a one-sided patriarchal system that the Bonannos and Profacis had lived under for generations."[6]

When Josephine got married, Bill Bonanno gained revenge by thinking up a way he had been "insulted" by her. Then he refused to attend her wedding, and refused to permit his wife, despite her pleas, to go to her own sister's wedding.

The movie would have been more realistic if it had presented the Italian women of Michael's generation as successfully striking out on their own to find American men who were secure in their professions and who knew nothing about subservient Sicilian wives. (This would also have allowed the female Italian characters to have some depth, some complexity—instead of being relegated to one-dimensional stereotypes.) For a moment's reflection would lead one to realize that the women of Michael's generation would be more likely to seek marital companionship outside the traditional fold than the men would.

Both *Godfather* films sentimentally enhance further the romantic glamor of the men in the Mafia by making the non-Mafia men weak, unattractive, at times repulsive. Connie Corleone "strays" from the fold only far enough to marry Rizzi, an Italian who is not originally part of the Mafia organization. He proves to be a gutless ninny who bullies his wife and fatally betrays his brother-in-law, Sonny. In *The Godfather, Part II* Connie woos and is courted by a WASP who, predictably, quickly proves to be a silly fop. By the time that the second film nears its end, Connie is—literally—on her knees in front of Michael confessing her weaknesses to him and praising him.

Their brother Freddie marries a non-subservient woman. She, predictably, is awful. Freddie, not the Mafia "type," is as weak as Connie's first husband; and Freddie betrays Michael. The most prominent WASP outsider in *Part II* is Senator Geary. He, predictably, is made more repulsive than all the Mafia hatchet-men put together.

The Godfather, in essence, is miles removed from a cold realistic look at the Mafia, at home or conducting "business." Andrew Sarris summed the matter up when he stated that the film is "about as unkind to the Mafia as *Mein Kampf* is to Adolf Hitler."[7]

If *The Godfather* is not a realistic depiction of the Mafia, one can only make a muddle of things by discussing the film version of the Mafia, the real Mafia, and the United States all in the same breath. Both Coppola and Brando, although intermittently admitting the movie-Mafia is a romanticized version, have tried to insist that the real Mafia and the United States are alike both fundamentally and in detail. Coppola said, "I feel that the Mafia is an incredible metaphor for this country."[8]

Perhaps the only reason this comparison received so much serious attention is that many, many Americans were thoroughly disgusted by American politics at the time *The Godfather* was shown throughout the land. These people included those who were eager to accept comparisons that denigrated the United States. There is no question that the United States is less pure than paradise. But most of the points of comparsion between the Mafia and the United States were much too general to apply solely to the American government. Simultaneously, basic differences between the two were obfuscated or simply ignored.

Brando, for instance, said that, like the Mafia, America engaged in "the killing of people." What nation has not done so? He said that the Mafia offers an example of "capitalists." Even if true, this hardly narrows the comparison down to the United States. In its pursuit of wealth, the Mafia could just as easily be compared with Genghis Khan. Drifting further away from a specific comparsion with the United States government, Brando said that "big business kills us all the time—with cars and cigarettes and pollution."[9] I would suggest that there is more than a little difference in speaking about a business company producing cigarettes that, if bought and smoked over a number of years, can adversely affect your health and speaking about a bunch of thugs who tell you that if you do not do today exactly what they want you to do, tonight they will murder you in a particularly gruesome way.

Asked if he agreed with Brando's viewpoint, Coppola replied, "Brando got that from me." Then Coppola elaborated. "Both the Mafia and America have roots in Europe . . . . Basically, both the Mafia and America feel they are benevolent organisations. Both the Mafia and America have their hands stained with blood from what it is necessary to do to protect their power and interests. Both are totally capitalistic phenomena and basically have a profit motive."[10]

To begin at the point where such a comparison should begin, the origin and development of the Mafia in America has very little similarity to the origin and development of American capitalism. In colonial America the Puritans came to believe that economic prosperity could be an indication that one was favored by God. Thus, sanction was given for pursuing property—by moral means. Gradually, for the non-Puritan the qualification "by moral means" was abandoned. Many of the multimillionaires of the nineteenth century *were* cold-hearted business men. But, unlike the Mafia, very few of these men ever broke the law. So, too, while the activities of the Mafia were parasitical and repressive, these millionaires helped the nation prosper (though that was by no means their primary goal).

The Mafia in America developed out of the sense of alienation felt by the Sicilian immigrants. These people wanted to prosper, but some of them did not want to struggle to prosper by legal means. They discovered that they could gain money and power by using the same strong-arm tactics that were used in "the old country." As Luigi Barzini stated in *The Italians*, these men "discovered that the ancient arts were far more useful in America and went farther. The Americans were generally trustful, unprepared to defend themselves from guile, often unwilling to fight for what they considered small stakes."[11] That is to say, the Mafia flourished not because its members were duplications of typical Americans, but because they were *so different* that Americans did not know how to cope with them.

It is true that, like the Mafia, America has been inspired by a profit motive. But so have all other nations, all businesses, and many individuals, including some in the movie industry of which Coppola is a part. It is true that both the Mafia and America have their roots in Europe. So do Shakespeare's plays, the steam engine, pasteurized milk, kissing under the mistletoe—and much else. To state that the Mafia feels itself to be a "benevolent" organization is just plain silly. Were Lucky Luciano and Joe "Bananas" Bonanno disappointed that they were never awarded a Nobel Peace Prize?

A Fine Gangster Film

If, finally, *The Godfather* is not more than a gangster film, it is, despite its flaws, one of the finest gangster films ever made.

Without question, one major reason for this achievement is the screenplay. On the whole, Puzo and Coppola did an excellent job of transferring the novel's story into a screenplay.

Some critics insisted that the novel was dreadful. Perhaps they wanted to emphasize the difference in quality between the book and the film in order to enhance the film, which they were eager to praise. Pauline Kael described the book as "trash" and "unreadable."[12]

The novel is certainly readable, nor is it trash really. Trashy literature is the pornography sold in the Times Square area or in Boston's "Combat Zone." At its poorest, the novel is pedestrian. The style is often flat, and sometimes clumsy. The characters, with rare exception, are stereotypes. Two of the main stories, concerning Johnny Fontane and (particularly) Lucy Mancini, are dull from beginning to end. Even the material about the most impressive characters, the Don and Michael, has its weak spots. The section on the Don's career between the time he rises to power in the "old neighborhood" and the time of his daughter's wedding is slow-moving. The section on Michael's stay in Sicily is sometimes tedious.

What is most interesting in the novel (and what keeps the reader turning the pages) is Puzo's presentation of what he has learned about the intricacies of the standard operations of a Mafia gang, or "family." The reader is gripped by the maneuverings of Don Corleone and his men, especially when warfare breaks out between his gang and rival gangs. The depiction of the domestic lives of these men, and of how this part of their lives intertwines with their "business" lives, is almost equally interesting. The reader wants to know all of the details that Puzo presents—and more. And he wants to know how the Don and his men will defeat their enemies.

The reader also enjoys the opportunity to have his cake and to eat it too. He is stirred, excited by the Don's and Michael's ultimate Mafia victory. Yet he is willingly steered into morally disapproving of Michael—especially at the end of the story when Kay lights a candle for Michael's soul. The reader is given two happy endings. Michael triumphs over his enemies, and Michael is morally condemned.

Yet, if Kael is guilty of exaggeration in her dismissal of the novel as trash, she hit the bull's-eye when she stated that "Puzo provided what Coppola needed: a storyteller's outpouring of incidents and details to choose from."[13] Gary Arnold, commenting on this same point, wrote, *"The Godfather* is an interesting and instinctive piece of collaboration, because Coppola and Puzo don't seem to have much in common. There's been a happy, miraculous accident: Coppola's exquisite sensibility refines the crudities out of Puzo's story, while that brutal, archetypal, melodramatic story concentrates and intensifies Coppola's abilities in a way the 'original' but vague *Rain People* never did."[14]

Although the plot of *You're A Big Boy Now* is adequate and cleverly intricate at times, the film is far more memorable for its characterizations. The superiority of character delineation to plot development in *The Rain People* is even starker. Coppola's screenplay for *The Conversation* also has serious weaknesses in its plot. It is true, then, that Puzo provided Coppola with what the latter has had much trouble providing himself with: a roaring good plot—and lots of it.

However, because Coppola both co-authored the screenplay and, as director, made the final decisions concerning the script, he should gain the bulk of the praise for turning the novel's material into a film that is better than the book. He must be praised in particular for the material he chose *not* to present on the screen. He deleted many, many things that were in the book. And he was right every time. The filmgoer should give thanks, for instance, that the Lucy Mancini plot was eliminated (she is a very minor character in the film), and that only some of the Johnny Fontane plot was retained—primarily, as Coppola later remarked, to set up the Don's defeat of Jack Woltz by means of decapitating Woltz's favorite horse.

Scenes from the book that made it difficult at times to consider the Don's gang as "the good guys" were also eliminated. Because Puzo stated that Coppola "softened" the Mafia characters in the film-script, Coppola must be given credit for not including such scenes as the calculated and vicious beating given Jerry Wagner and Kevin Moonan (a "favor" the Don does for the undertaker Amerigo Bonasera), or the fatal beating Albert Neri inflicted, a beating that lost him his position on the police force, but spurred the Don to hire him, or the scene in which Luca Brasi, working for the Don, takes an ax and chops up another gunman from feet to head. On a movie screen, scenes presenting such brutality by the Don's men—no matter *what* the justification—would have prevented the audience from identifying with and rooting for the Don and Michael.

This would have been especially true concerning the beating of Wagner and Moonan, for this occurs quite early in the story— before the audience could commit itself to the Corleones. In the film, Bonasera asks the Don to kill the two young men. The stress in the scene is on the Don's chastising Bonasera for desiring such an excessive punishment.

Still, the members of the movie audience who had not read *The Godfather* before seeing the film version encountered a few problems that the screenplay did not solve. At times it was not at all clear which dark, heavy-set men were members of which gang. Consequently, the violent acts committed by these men were confusing. Another serious flaw for the filmgoer ignorant of the novel—but well aware that superstar Brando, as Don Corleone, had been given the largest share of the advertising—is the film's sudden shift of attention to Michael (one of several characters quickly presented in the first long sequence), a shift that is more than a little startling. A swift readjustment must be made. The screenplay should have forsaken the novel's format enough to highlight Michael more in the opening scenes. It was right to keep Michael on the fringes of the action, but he should not have been allowed to be on the fringes of the filmgoer's consciousness.

There were other script problems. In the movie—though not in the novel—Don Corleone is basically a static character. None of his early life is shown until *The Godfather, Part II* appeared. In the first film the Don does not develop as a character. He is shown only near the end of his career. Thus, the pace of the movie at the start is a touch too slow. (Pace, as we have seen, is often a problem for Coppola.)

In both the book and the film-script, the Sicilian sequence is unimpressive. In the novel this segment has only one value. Puzo uses the segment to make interesting comments on the origin, development, and present activities of the Sicilian Mafia. Next to none of this was included in the screenplay. Quite sentimental, the movie sequence does bring the audience closer to Michael and complete the audience's adjustment to Michael's gaining the spotlight. But the audience could have adjusted perhaps even more easily if Michael's greater involvement in Mafia business had been presented sooner. There would have been time to do this if the Sicilian sequence had been pruned.

Michael's background preceding his involvement in his father's Mafia activities is almost as unconvincing in the film as it is in the novel. The audience is told that Michael attended college and served in the armed forces. But neither experience has had any discernible effect on him. His life in the armed forces made no impression at all on his character. Nor is there anything about him that indicates he worked for and received a superior education.

What we have here is a phony attempt to increase the "drama" of Michael's gradual involvement in Mafia operations by intensifying the disparity between what Michael—so "different" from the rest of the family—once was (and might have gone on to be) and what he becomes. It is an exciting idea. But no effort was expended to make the point believable (if it ever *could* have been made believable). It is most fortunate that the audience quickly becomes so interested in Michael's present actions and character development that it just as quickly stops caring about Michael's past life.

On the other hand, the screenplay decisively improves on the relationship between Michael and Kay Adams. The portrait of Kay in the book is dismal. Perhaps because Puzo did not know much about non-Catholic women such as Kay, she remains almost totally unreal in the book, even though she receives a fair amount of Puzo's attention—more attention than she receives in the film. (The other female characters in the book are types of Italian women that Puzo obviously was more familiar with and could depict with some confidence.)

The screenplay cleverly undercuts the problem of Kay's thinness as a character by making Michael more aggressive in his pursuit of Kay than he was in the book (where Kay does most of the pursuing). The scene in which Michael seeks Kay out after he returns from

Sicily is an excellent dramatization of the tension and the tenderness interlaced in their love for each other. This shift in plot also fits in better with Michael's otherwise forceful character—and succeeds in making Michael more attractive.

The individual improvements that Coppola, aided by Puzo and Towne, made in various segments of the story do not, however, wholly account for the high quality of the film. Another reason the movie version succeeds is that Coppola utilizes the potential of the ganster-film genre so well. Stanley J. Solomon singled out and stressed this basic point. He stated, "As immoral as crime may be in the abstract, in a particular film it is usually measured against an even less appealing alternative. As a result the criminal act performed by the main character in comparison to what others are doing in the same film often creates the necessary sympathy on the part of the audience . . . . In Francis Ford Coppola's *The Godfather*, we side with one gang against all its opposition not because we approve of the gang's murders, but because the opposing criminal factions are more chaotic, less scrupulous, and apparently less skillful at organizational crime."

Solomon added, "The overwhelming popular success of *The Godfather* seems attributable not only to the recent great public interest in organized crime, but also to the film's total artistic exploitation of the patterns of its genre. That these conventions should strike audiences and critics as new . . . testifies to Coppola's skill in combining the most interesting elements of the genre's various relevant categories—criminal organizations, gangsters, gang wars, and syndicate operations."[15]

One more feature of *The Godfather* that operates with outstanding success within the format of the gangster film must be added to the list of those already specified and praised, and that is Coppola's presentation of violence. Curiously enough, Coppola—perhaps because of his personal ideology—has not always been comfortable with the praise that has come to him for his successful—powerful—presentation of violence. He once commented that "if the picture seems to some to be irresponsible because it celebrates violence, that was never my intent. In fact, there's very little actual violence in the film. It occurs very quickly. It's just that the violence happens to characters you like."[16]

This is simply not true. Rather early in the movie, for instance, Luca Brasi—a character the audience not only does not particularly like, but barely can identify as a member of the Don's gang—is slowly choked to death. Brasi dies in a manner even a bit more grisly than he does in the book. In the latter, an enemy grabs one of his arms, another enemy grabs the other, and a third garrots him. In the movie, one of Brasi's hands is first impaled by a knife to the top of the bar. This renders one arm helpless and makes his strangulation even more appalling—and riveting.

Actually, the film is saturated with a combination of the threat of violence, the plans to commit violence, the fear of violence, the actual committing of violence, and the repercussions to acts of violence. The basic reason that one keeps watching the movie, even when there are slow spots or irritating confusions, is that the story centers literally on life-and-death struggles. No other film has so imaginatively presented murder in such a variety of visually vivid ways. Who, for example, could ever forget the sight of Carlo Rizzi kicking a hole in the car windshield as he tries to break free from the man choking him to death? or the sight of Brasi's impaled hand? or the bullet hole in McCluskey's head when Michael shoots McCluskey and Sollozzo? or the bullet-shattered eyeglasses worn by Moe Greene, another Corleone enemy?

Yet, to applaud Coppola for his contributions to the screenplay and his utilization of the gangster-film genre is not to have exhausted the reasons he should be praised for his work on *The Godfather*. He should, finally, also be commended for helping the actors fulfill their considerable potential. Coppola's work here demonstrates yet again his exceptional ability to elicit quality performances. Only one of the major performances proves disappointing, and that one has been much praised and honored.

The majority of critics thought all the major roles were handled in excellent fashion and singled out Marlon Brando for special praise. Indeed, after receiving so many lukewarm or hostile critical reviews for almost all of his screen appearances for a good number of years, Brando was almost hysterically applauded for his portrayal of Don Corleone. In some instances, this might have been another case of the critics, after having gone far in one direction, changing their mood and deciding to swing back in the opposite direction and extol the artist they had so long lambasted.

As Coppola's estimate would have it, Brando is one of the finest living actors. Brando's earliest screen performances were highly, and validly, praised. For *Viva Zapata!* Brando has not been, in fact, praised highly enough. The film, principally because of Brando, is extraordinarily good. Other films such as *A Streetcar Named Desire* and *On the Waterfront,* seen twenty years after their initial release, reveal that Brando's performances hold up solidly. His brilliance astonishes the viewer all over again. Some of the work he did in later films is just as good. He gave one of his greatest performances in *Reflections in a Golden Eye,* a movie that most critics wholly rejected. He created a very interesting character in *The Young Lions*—although the character severely undercut the theme and the dramatic development of the story.

As the years went on, however, Brando not only distorted the plots of some of the movies he appeared in by altering the character he played, but he also began drawing the attention of the audience *not* to his character, but to his attempts to play the character. And this was the case with his performance in *The Godfather.*

One only intermittently becomes interested in, drawn toward, the character that Brando plays. All too frequently, when Brando is on the screen, the viewer is distracted by his awareness that Brando is trying to play the part of Don Corleone.

The major problem is Brando's voice. One is very conscious of Brando's straining his vocal cords to—for some strange reason—give Corleone a high-pitched, thin voice. His voice is continually distracting. Furthermore, he speaks so tediously slowly.

The "strange reason" for all this was provided only well after the film was released. Shortly before filming began, Coppola played a tape recording of Frank Costello's voice for the benefit of Brando. Costello's high-pitched voice fascinated Brando; and, encouraged by Coppola, he decided to imitate it. In his later appearances in the film his voice climbs still higher in tone. "This was to indicate that he had been shot in the throat during his near-assassination; Coppola admitted afterward that he had erred in neglecting to establish the fact."[17]

Stanley Kauffmann was one critic who did not get on the Brando bandwagon. Kauffmann wrote that "from his opening line, with his back toward us, Brando betrays that he hasn't even got the man's voice under control. (Listen to the word 'first.' Pure Brando, not Corleone.) Insecurity and assumption streak the job from then on. They have put padding in his checks and dirtied his teeth, he speaks hoarsely and moves stiffly, and these combined mechanics are hailed as great acting . . . . His resident power, his sheer innate force, has rarely seemed weaker . . . . What Brando manufactures is surface—studied but easy effects."[18]

The film is too long; and—by far—the majority of sections that drag are the sections that feature Brando. One cause of this was cited earlier: Don Corleone is too static a character in this first of two films that feature his life story. But another reason is that Brando's performance slows the momentum of the movie to the proverbial snail's pace.

On the other hand, no one should stint in his praise for the other actors. Al Pacino is excellent. Although he is only on the fringe of the action at first, he gradually and adroitly conveys to the audience that he embodies outstanding potential power—strength, decisiveness, and shrewdness. For this reason the audience is convinced by Michael's capable handling of the situation, fraught with danger, at the hospital. Pacino's Michael is not a static character. He changes, matures (for better and for worse) right before our eyes.

It is Pacino who is responsible for the hospital sequence being the first superb sequence in the film. The same thing is true, of course, in the sequence in which Michael irrevocably alters the course of his adult life—the sequence culminating in his killing McCluskey and Sollozzo. It is Pacino, tense, barely able to breathe, in the bathroom reaching for the gun who, primarily, makes that sequence almost unbearably gripping.

There are quick touches too. Although the Sicilian section dragged, Pacino has a magnificent moment late in that section. It occurs when Michael's first wife, Apollonia, prepares to start the car. As she does so, Michael's face undergoes several distinct, rapid changes of expression as he senses that his enemies have rigged the car with a bomb. The final insight comes, we see, as quick as a fingersnap—though just an instant too late to save his wife's life.

Other performers also excelled. James Caan certainly proved that Jimmie Kilgannon, the mentally-maimed, slow-talking athlete in *The Rain People*, was only one kind of character he could play. As Sonny Corleone, Caan was not given much variety of material to work with, but he did admirably within the confines of the script. When Sonny was not exploding into violence, it was obvious, thanks to Caan, that Sonny's taut nerves, abundant energy, and latent anger were ready to coalesce in violence. Sonny even engages in sexual intercourse violently—by pinning his mistress Lucy Mancini up against a door. We are equally well prepared to believe Sonny would blunder at the business discussion, blurt out his willingness to deal in drugs, and, later, blunder into a trap that costs him his life.

Robert Duvall portrayed Tom Hagen, a character who could have faded into the wallpaper because he plays no direct part in the violence. In the hands of Duvall, however, Hagen serves as a link between the audience and the Corleone family. Hagen is the non-Italian "outsider" who is nevertheless on the inside. Duvall does an especially good job when he is kidnapped. He dramatically portrays the worry and nervousness Hagen feels, but he never lets the part become melodramatic.

As the corrupt and hardened McCluskey, Sterling Hayden is another big reason that the sequence culminating in Michael's killing of Sollozzo and McCluskey is so gripping. McCluskey's grim badgering of Michael intensifies the audience's hunger for Michael to gain revenge; and this badgering is the result of Hayden's tough chiseled face, intimidating body, and grating voice.

Diane Keaton is excellent in conveying Kay's emotional confusion. One watches, fascinated, the expression of Kay's intense yearning for Michael, yet her ceaseless uncertainty about him. She is rarely, if ever, at ease with him, sure of him, even when he is reassuring her. Keaton manages to make her whole body hunger for Michael, yet hold back.

Although many scenes and whole sequences have been mentioned and praised during the discussion about the contributions made to the film by Coppola, Puzo, and the actors, a few more could be mentioned. The morning scene in which Jack Woltz gradually, groggily, realizes that there is blood on the sheets and that the blood comes from the severed head of his favorite horse is superbly rendered. It vividly convinces us that we are indeed viewing the lives of men who want their own way. The murder attempt while the Don is buying fruit is expertly executed. Brando resisted an impulse that a lesser actor would have followed—the impulse to press the material too hard and ham it up. Brando also succeeds in the Don's deeply touching death scene. The scene is as good as Coppola came to believe it was.

Concerning the conclusion of the film, Stephen Farber remarked, "When Michael's wife Kay asks him if he had anything to do with the murder of his sister's husband, he lies to her, comforting her with the patronizing affection one would show a child. She leaves the room, but sees the other mafiosi come in to pay tribute to their new godfather. Kay stares, puzzled and horrified, then the door is closed and the screen goes to black; we feel she is excluded forever from everything important in her husband's life."[19] This leads us away from this fine motion picture and points toward the sequel.

Coppola, disappointed that many members of the audience failed to grasp the moral implications of the film's ending, later commented, "I felt I was making a harsh statement about the Mafia and power at the end of *Godfather I* when Michael murders all those people, then lies to his wife and closes the door. But obviously, many people didn't get the point I was making. And so if the statement I was trying to make was outbalanced by the charismatic aspects of the characters, I felt *Godfather II* was an opportunity to rectify that."[20]

8

"A Conversation In Private"

THE ENORMOUS SUCCESS of *The Godfather* brought Coppola the kind of financial wealth many people dream about, but never come anywhere near obtaining. It also created new pressures. Coppola remarked, "I'm resentful that people all say, 'Do you think you can top *The Godfather?*' I know I could never top it in terms of financial success, and I don't even intend to try." Then he specified what his new goal was. "I do want to make a film that tops it as a really moving human document. It's like some music I hear once in a while. I hear it and I think 'Why can't I make a film that feels like that?' That's what I'm going to try to do. I don't know that I'll be able to pull it off."

He also commented on what partially bred his preoccupation with making "modest films about contemporary human situations," films such as *The Rain People* and *The Conversation*. He explained, "I started getting interested in movies in the 1950s. And that's just the period when Ingmar Bergman and Federico Fellini were being talked about. So I don't know to what extent my desire to do that kind of film dates back to a time when I was very impressionable and thought, 'That's art.' "[1]

So, before he became totally caught up in the *Godfather* material for a second time, Coppola worked on a variety of other projects, including *The Conversation*. He directed Noel Coward's *Private Lives* for the American Conservatory Theatre in San Francisco right after he finished his work on the first *Godfather* film. It was a project done in a hurry; and he felt lucky when the production, despite dress rehearsal problems, turned out satisfactorily. Then he spent a month creating a screenplay out of Fitzgerald's *The Great Gatsby*, though the final film version did not reach the public for another two years.

While working intermittently on new and revised material for

127

Gene Hackman (Harry Caul) in The Conversation
Credit: The Museum of Modern Art/Film Stills Archive

The Conversation, Coppola staged the American première of Gottfried von Einem's *The Visit of the Old Lady* for the San Francisco Opera Company. His main reason for taking on this task was an understandable one. After having worked day after day under intense pressure to make *The Godfather*, Coppola explained, "I needed something different, something where I could experiment more freely, without political or financial pressures."

Staging the opera proved to be a learning experience for Coppola more than a passing on of his accumulated knowledge. During the first run-through, a week before opening night, he discovered that much of the previous work he had done with the singers was a waste of time. "I realized that nearly all the intimate detail I had been working on simply got lost. I had given the chorus members individual bits to do, for instance, like in the wedding scene in *The Godfather*. But at the run-through, from that distance, they all merged into a mob. Things get lost in opera, and music slows time down. It's simply not a natural art form, so you have to bring in stylization."[2]

Nonetheless, the première was a moderate success. Coppola talked immediately about his desire to stage *Turandot*, but this project was postponed indefinitely.

Along with two friends, Peter Bogdanovich and William Friedkin (director of *The French Connection*), Coppola created the Directors Company. Conceived by Coppola and Charles Bluhdorn, chairman of Gulf & Western Industries, Directors Company was owned by the three directors and by Paramount (owned by Gulf & Western). Bogdanovich, Friedkin, and Coppola agreed to direct four films over a twelve-year period, films which Paramount would distribute. In return, Paramount would provide up to $31,500,000 to finance these films. One of Bogdanovich's biggest hits, *Paper Moon*, was released within this framework.

Coppola played a still more important part in the making of *American Graffiti*, an extremely successful movie. Coppola's close friend George Lucas had worked on this project for some time. But when Lucas felt the film was ready for production, he could not interest any of the big studios in financing it. The script was turned down almost a dozen times.

When Universal rejected the project, Coppola met with studio officials. Afterwards, the studio agreed to supply the almost one million dollars Lucas asked for. In return, Coppola agreed to serve as executive producer and to direct a film at the studio. As a reward for his commitment to *American Graffiti*, Coppola requested and was granted a percentage of the movie's profits—which turned out to be considerable.

Lucas later stated that his film would not have gotten into production if it had not been for Coppola. Furthermore, when it became clear that the film needed reediting, heavy pressure was put on Lucas to reedit it in ways he strongly disapproved of. Once more, Coppola rescued his friend. Coppola's intervention "allowed Lucas to make the film he wanted to make."[3]

On March 27, 1973 Coppola appeared before all the television viewers who were watching the Academy Awards ceremony. *The Godfather* was voted the best film of 1972. Coppola won an Oscar for co-writing the script. Marlon Brando also won one for his portrayal of Don Corleone.

The fact that Coppola and several other young directors had attended (or at least had some connection with) film-school programs now became big news. Coppola's name was usually given special priority in articles about film schools because he had made the most financially successful movie of all those that the film-school "group" had directed. But attention also came to George Lucas, John Milius (director of *Dillinger*), John Hancock (*Bang the Drum Slowly*), Martin Scorsese (*Mean Streets*), and Noel Black (*Pretty Poison*). Scorsese remarked, "For a while film schools seemed to have a stigma" attached to them. But when movies made by ex-students became both financial and critical successes, snide comments about "student pretensions" dropped away.[4]

The Conversation

It was at this time that Coppola began to concentrate on *The Conversation*. He spoke to movie critic Marjorie Rosen at great length about the development of this project. The idea for the script originated in 1967–1968. Coppola recalled, "I've always been interested in technology of all kinds . . . . I was having a conversation with Irvin Kershner, the director; we were talking about surveillance. He mentioned that the safest place for two people who wanted to have a conversation in private would be outside in a crowd. Then he added that he had heard of microphones that had gun sights on them that were so powerful and selective that they could, if aimed at the mouths of these people in the crowd, pick up their conversation." Coppola immediately envisioned "two people walking through a crowd with their conversation being interrupted every time someone steps in front of the gunsight."

He did not finish the script until 1969. He more or less finished rewriting it again shortly before he started work on the shooting of the film. Over the years he shifted the main focus of attention away from the targets of the eavesdropping to the eavesdropper. He did not, however, alter the script because of the early Watergate news. He told Rosen, "The actual break-in . . . was not considered a big deal at the time. It happened around the time we were shooting the warehouse scene, which is about two-thirds through the movie. We knew about it, but we never knew it was of such significance." But, he added, "Generally for the last few years, I had been aware of any stories that had to do with eavesdropping, looking for little details that might be good. The political references in the picture, which are very slight, are all in the old script. It's just a matter of common sense that if people were using tapes to bug business companies, they would be using it in political elections."

If some people felt that the Watergate findings and publicity must have increased interest in *The Conversation*, Coppola felt otherwise. "I almost think that the picture would have been better received had Watergate not happened. Now, you can look at it, even if you know it was written before Watergate and say, 'Oh, look at that. Of course, well, sure.'"

According to Rosen's interview, several influences were at work on Coppola when he made this film. Because he thought the film was a "thriller" to some extent, he was quite conscious of Alfred Hitchcock's movies. "Anyone who intends to make a film in the thriller genre is a student of Hitchcock," he stated. "He invented it. I began to realize that the only way I could get the money to do this picture would be if it worked on some level other than just an inquiry into [Harry Caul]. I didn't think that anybody would go see a movie that was just a mundane story of just a wiretapper. I felt, very early on, that it had to be a kind of horror film—a Hitchcockian horror film. I reviewed the Hitchcock films and tried to understand why they work so well."

This scrutiny led Coppola to an unexpected conclusion. "I think I'm a lot different from Hitchcock in my approach. Hitchcock seems to be almost entirely interested in the design of his films. I'm much more interested in performances. I don't care for most Hitchcock films because they're terribly acted."

A stronger influence on Coppola was the French director Henri-Georges Clouzot. "I identify much more with Clouzot, who works not only on a thriller level but has some other matter to his films. I remember, when I was in high school, *Diabolique* was showing. If anything, I would hope that *The Conversation* would have that kind of effect."

Another influence, interestingly enough, was Hermann Hesse. "I was reading *Steppenwolf* at the time I wrote *The Conversation*, and I was very impressed with this kind of character, Harry Horner. Hence, my guy's name is Harry. He lives alone in an apartment like the character in *Steppenwolf.*"

Coppola stressed to Rosen various experiments that he tried while making the film. The use of sound in the movie was one. Coppola worked very closely with Walter Murch, who, like Lucas, had attended the film-school program at University of Southern California. Murch did the sound for *The Rain People, THX-1138, American Graffiti,* and *The Godfather*. Coppola remarked, "As I was writing [*The Conversation*], I had in mind that Walter would do the sound. So I wrote many scenes to be sound-oriented, like a murder occurring in another room that you don't see but you hear."

Coppola experimented with the presentation of two characters by means of a conversation that is recorded. He explained that movies "are all made the same way and the reason they're made the same way is because the audiences want them that way. The films cost so much that to really veer from that way of telling a story, you have to be independently wealthy and subsidize it." Still, in *The Conversation* he tried a new approach to character delineation.

That his approach went unrecognized, never mind unrewarded, annoyed him. "I read a review of *The Conversation* that describes the two characters, the boy and the girl walking, as skimpily drawn. Well, here I am deliberately trying to not unveil their characters in a conventional way. I'm trying to give you an impression of their characters. The only film on those two characters is the same dumb conversation. It's my attempt at trying to find another way to give character to an audience instead of just a classic playwright's way of giving you a little background and unveil traits and show you the contradictions. I'm just showing you the same moment over and over. I'm using repetition instead of exposition. The second I do it, someone says it's skimpy."[5]

Coppola might also have been consciously trying to reveal facets of his own personality through his main character Harry Caul. Al Pacino once commented, "Francis is an emotional voyeur. He looks, he sees, he watches people's emotions. He can't help it."[6] Caul, portrayed by Gene Hackman, is more than a little like this.

As *The Conversation* begins, the camera shows us a park, Union Square in San Francisco. The camera moves in. We hear a combo playing "Red Red Robin." We see a young couple, played by Cindy Williams and Frederic Forrest, as well as Harry Caul. It quickly becomes clear that Harry, aided by three other men and an extraordinary amount of mechanical equipment, is attempting to record the couple's conversation.

When the young man and young woman leave the park, Harry returns to his apartment. He is startled to discover that during his absence the superintendent of the building had entered his apartment; Harry thought he had the only key to it. The next day, he goes to his office, located in an otherwise abandoned warehouse, and gradually assembles most of the couple's conversation on one clear tape.

That evening, he visits Amy, the woman whom he financially supports. But he becomes increasingly irritated when she asks him a few questions, and he abruptly leaves her apartment. Still tense the next day, he refuses to give the final tape to an assistant of the man, a "Director," who employed Harry to make the original tapes. The assistant warns Harry not to get involved. Harry takes the tape back to the warehouse and strives, successfully, to render audible one section of the conversation previously indistinct. This section includes the young man's remark, "He'd kill us if he got a chance."

Upset, Harry goes to confession and blurts out to the priest that a past assignment he completed ultimately led to the death of at least two people. Yet he insists, "I'm in no way responsible." He attends a convention featuring surveillance equipment and meets Bernie Moran, who considers Harry his only superior in their field. The Director's assistant shows up at the convention and tells Harry that the Director himself will accept the tape from Harry on Sunday. Harry replies, "I'll think about it."

That night he invites several people, including Moran and a

prostitute, Meredith, to the warehouse for a party. Meredith stays behind. She and Harry have sex; then Harry falls asleep. He dreams that he meets the girl and attempts, more and more intensely, to explain himself to her by describing his past life, particularly his boyhood years.

When he awakens, Meredith and his tapes are gone. After he returns to his apartment, the assistant phones him. Harry is shocked to learn that despite his nervous efforts to keep his private life a secret, the assistant has a complete dossier on him. The assistant also tells him that the Director had the tapes stolen because he was afraid Harry might destroy them. Harry is instructed to come to the Director's office on Sunday to pick up his money.

On the tapes, the couple refer to a meeting between the Director and themselves at a hotel on that same Sunday. Although Harry takes his fee, he is very concerned about the couple's welfare. He rents the hotel apartment next to the apartment where the rendez-vous is to take place and sets up his equipment. When the sounds from the next apartment become loud and violent, Harry jumps into bed and pulls the covers over his head. Hours later, he uses a skeleton key to let himself into the next apartment, which appears neat and tidy. Prompted by an intuition, he flushes the toilet. Blood and blood-soaked rags float to the surface and spill onto the floor.

Harry hurries back to the Director's office building, but is turned away. Later, pausing at a newstand, he reads the headlines which declare that the Director was killed in an auto accident. He now realizes that he completely misinterpreted the conversation on the tapes. He thought the couple feared that the Director was going to kill them, but they, in fact, were planning to murder the Director.

Back in his apartment, Harry is told over the phone that, because of what he knows, he is being kept under surveillance. Frantic, he starts searching for bugging devices. He pulls apart the whole apartment—even the walls and floor, but he fails to find anything. At last he gives up and sits in his bare apartment playing the saxophone.

Analysis

In May, 1974, *The Conversation* was awarded the Cannes Film Festival's highest prize, the Golden Palm. When it was released in the United States it received high praise from many critics, but it was not a financial success. Stanley Kauffmann described it as "interesting," "satisfying," and treating a serious subject "with extraordinary cinematic skill."[7] Gerald Mast referred to it as the first of Coppola's films to reveal his "social conscience and intellectual consciousness."[8]

Thematically, the film is powerful. By concentrating on one character, Harry Caul, an expert in the field of surveillance, it probes the question of responsibility concerning modern professions which at first glance seem wholly technical and amoral.

Caul, aware that some people would disapprove of his professional activities on moral grounds, tries to convince himself his work is morally neutral. To do this, he strives to remain ignorant about his employers, about the people he spies on, and about the human consequences resulting from the information he gathers. This narrow, negative goal makes his whole life increasingly sterile. He comes to believe that he must protect his private life from the same kind of intrusions he perpetrates in his work. He cuts himself off from other people in his private life just as he cuts himself off from learning too much about his employers and his victims.

Like almost all the other screenplays Coppola has written, the script for *The Conversation* features a character study. In its best scenes the movie offers several facets of the main character's potentially interesting life. But the movie is also a criticism of certain traits in the typical American.

David Denby stated that *The Conversation* attacks a way of thinking that is "a natural product of American business values and our eternal boyish enthusiasm for technology as an end in itself." Referring to the scenes at the convention and the post-convention party, Denby wrote, "Coppola has a savagely good time with Harry's surveillance colleagues. Boastful, frenetic, absurdly aggressive, these American go-getters can't stop competing for a moment, not even at a party, and so they begin showing off and playing dirty tricks on one another. Their viciousness while 'relaxing', more revealing than any amount of overt skulduggery, suggests that they are successful precisely because they don't give a damn who they hurt or how much. The code of 'professionalism' provides an apparent morality, a blinding justification for any act; they have no idea, not even a suspicion, that they are evil men."[9]

The convention is one of the best sequences in the film. Particularly startling is that this kind of convention is completely out in the open, in vivid contrast to the professional activities of the men who utilize the surveillance equipment flashily advertised at the convention. Except for the occasions during the opening sequence in which Caul and his assistants leave their truck full of equipment in order to make sure that they can pick up the conversation of the couple strolling around Union Square, Caul operates only within sealed-off areas. These confined quarters set up still more dramatically the shock of the convention's wide-openness.

But the most powerful part of this sequence is that—without one word being said about the point—the wide-openness emphasizes the conventioneers' belief that there is absolutely nothing wrong with the activities they engage in. On behalf of the surveillance men who hide in order to spy, the convention says, paradoxically, "We have nothing to hide and, so, nothing to be ashamed of."

It is, however, the character of Harry Caul, not the film's social-political implications, that stirs the viewer's interest the most. Still, it should be kept in mind that the secondary motif is by no means totally separated from the major motif. Harry's last name is also the word used to describe the membrane sometimes found on a new-born baby's face. Such a caul has been considered an omen, a sign that the baby will grow up to be a prophet or leader of his tribe. It is an interesting and ironic implication that Harry Caul may be a precursor of the ultimate modern man.

Caul's dominant trait is his desire to suppress his humanity, his human self. He doggedly tries to limit all his relationships. He not only lies about his age to Amy, his female companion ("mistress" is too strong a term to indicate their relationship), he does not even tell her in advance the date of his birthday. He never relaxes with Amy enough to take off his plastic raincoat—even during their lovemaking. (He, in fact, wears his raincoat for "protection" on the sunniest of days.) He rushes into Amy's apartment, ready to catch her doing something she should not do—and "catches" her eating a piece of candy. When she asks him a few innocuous questions, he becomes very angry and stalks out of the apartment—while she tells him that she will not wait for his visits any more.

He is cold toward his right-hand man Stan. He rebuffs Stan's simplest questions. He chews Stan out over trivial matters, such as Stan's muttering a curse word. Later at the convention, he finds that

Stan has gone to work for someone else. Caul's obsessive secrecy is the reason for this. Stan tells Caul that he quit because Caul would never teach him anything about surveillance techniques.

Caul does not even play his saxophone with a group of other musicians. He sits alone in his apartment and "accompanies" recorded renditions of other musicians' work—except at the end of the movie when, after having pulled apart his tape-recording equipment in his search for a hidden microphone, he plays totally by himself. Caul's utter isolation in this final scene starkly contrasts the film's opening sequence, which features a lively combo playing in Union Square—that is, playing together, playing outdoors, and playing for all passersby to hear.

Nor does Caul's religion give any sustenance. When he goes to confession, he tries only to avoid communicating anything serious to the priest and to avoid self-confrontation. After he does blurt out something revealing, he immediately denies any serious significance to what he said. In the film's final sequence, when he is looking for the hidden microphone, he cannot at first bring himself to take apart the image of the Virgin Mary he has on the living room shelf. However, when his continued efforts to find the microphone fail, he rips the statue apart.

Only in the dream sequence does Harry come close to confronting himself and confessing his attempt to suppress his human self. He tells the silent figure of the young woman he spied on in the park that, while a youngster, he almost drowned once—and was disappointed that he had not drowned. In his present life, he is near "drowning" again.

His mounting dilemma, however, has been bred precisely because he has suppressed, but not managed to destroy, his human self. Caul's attitude early in the film indicates that he is wound up tight, and that whatever it is he has suppressed year after year is soon going to explode. While Stan and he are inside the "camouflaged" truck listening to the couple's conversation, two teen-age girls, unaware that what appears to them to be a mirror-like surface is actually a secret window, use the "mirror" to help them apply their lipstick. Stan is amused and snaps pictures of the girls. Instantly Caul rebukes him. In Caul's opinion, Stan should solely and somberly concentrate on doing a good job on the assignment. When Stan asks Caul what the latter thinks the assignment is

all about, Caul refuses to speculate. He snaps, "I don't want to know
. . . . All I want is a nice fat recording."

Back home after this day's work, Caul opens several door locks,
enters his apartment, and discovers a bottle of wine, a birthday
present, inside the apartment. He is totally uninterested in the
bottle as gift. Rather, he is upset to learn that, despite his increasingly paranoid efforts to cut himself off from others, another person
can enter his apartment. He is still vulnerable.

The scene with Amy further dramatizes the confusion, doubt, and
conflict in Caul. Amy happens to sing a few words of "Red Red
Robin," the same song the young woman in the park sang snatches
of. Caul immediately becomes suspicious of Amy. Even more interesting, Caul later confesses that the girl in the park reminded
him of Amy. He will not allow himself to become emotionally involved with Amy; he will not pursue her further when, later, he
phones her only to be told that her number has been changed. Yet
he *will* let himself become seriously involved in trying to protect
someone who reminds him of Amy.

Caul's turmoil peaks when he becomes irrationally suspicious of
his employer's assistant. Soon we learn the past event that first
caused Caul to be no longer able to separate his work from a moral
framework. At the post-convention party, Moran brings up the fact
that when Caul was operating in New York, he worked on an assignment that ultimately led to the murders of at least two people.
Caul quickly insists he was in no way responsible for what happened. Yet he did, right afterwards, move from New York to San
Francisco. He blotted out his past so completely that Stan, also at
the party, is surprised to learn only now that Caul ever worked in
New York.

When Moran suggests that Caul and he join forces, Caul emphatically insists, "I don't need anybody." Then, after everyone except
Meredith leaves, Caul begins to play the tapes again. He is now
thoroughly emotionally entangled in the couple's lives. On the tape
the young man mentions that they are walking in circles. So, too,
Caul keeps circling back to the couple. The young woman comments on a forlorn panhandler stretched out on a bench; juxtaposed
to this is a shot of Caul stretched out on his cot listening to the
comment.

By the time Caul rents the apartment next to the one where the couple will meet the Director, he is a confused, pitiful man. When the violence in the other apartment erupts, Caul cannot take it. He "hides" by pulling the bedsheets over his head. He is a scared little boy who has always hidden from life.

What is effectively dramatized by the climactic switch—in which the young couple kill the Director, rather than the reverse—is a sad paradox. Caul has become an expert at recording what human beings say to each other. But because he has tried, albeit unsuccessfully, to cut himself off from the rest of humanity, he is hopelessly ignorant about how to interpret, to understand the meaning of the words human beings say to each other.

Caul had thought originally that the boy in Union Square said, "He'd *kill* us if he got the chance." Only after the murder takes place does Caul realize that what the boy said was, "He'd kill *us* if *he* got the chance." This crucial misinterpretation is one of the finest dramatic ironies in all of the films Coppola has directed.

Because of *The Conversation*'s unusual plot and severely limited point of view, the only performer given much chance to show his ability is Gene Hackman. And even Hackman is limited by a character who has narrowed his life to so little. Within the stark confines of the character he portrays, Hackman does a commendable job. Denied—for better or for worse—a matinee idol's handsomeness, Hackman looks like a Harry Caul. He subtly makes it clear that Caul is slowly going to pieces. His face is taut, flushed. He makes nervous, fidgety gestures. He is irascible, becomes suddenly angry, and then pulls back from his anger. Hackman prepares us to see this "bright boy"—when it comes to gadgets—overwhelmed by the harsher and more complex aspects of reality. We fully accept that the violence he overhears in the next apartment would cause him to retreat, to hide under the bedsheets.

Unfortunately, despite the film's thematic levels, the effectiveness of individual scenes, and Hackman's polished performance, *The Conversation* is ultimately not a successful movie.

One major problem is that Coppola and Hackman failed to make Harry Caul a striking enough character to hold the audience's attention continuously. Coppola never completely solved the problem of how to convey the essential facets of Caul's character and what bred that character. Coppola said later, "It's very tricky to deal with a man who is your main character who you're watching for two hours or whatever the life of the film is, that doesn't talk to anybody, who lives alone, and who doesn't relate to anybody. I had given myself a very difficult assignment."[10]

Caul plays it *so* close to the vest that one becomes fatigued by the effort of trying—and usually failing—to find out what makes him tick. Caul all too often succeeds in concealing himself, in wrapping himself in a blandness as close-fitting as his plastic raincoat. In a word, he succeeds in being dull.

He opens up a bit while talking with Meredith at the party. But in this scene in particular the soundtrack is frequently almost inaudible. In fact at the Boston theater presenting *The Conversation*, before the showing of the film began, a recorded announcement declared that previous audiences had complained about being unable to hear what was said in certain scenes and the management wanted to make it clear that the fault was not in the theater's equipment. (Penelope Gilliatt, writing for the *New Yorker*, started her review by stating that a similar problem existed at the theater where she saw the film.) But even when all of Caul's words in this scene are heard, they are so cryptic they do not provide the audience with much useful information.

The only scene that effectively reveals some deeper aspects of Caul is the dream sequence. However, this scene clearly seems to be an act of desperation on Coppola's part, a scene forced into the film in order somehow to get *some* personal information about Caul across to the audience. It appears contrived because it comes right out of the blue. It could have been made plausible. Caul was building toward an emotional upheaval at least as far back as the time he learned that one job he did led to other people's deaths. If we had been shown even snatches of earlier "bad" dreams that Caul had, we would have been quite prepared for the extended dream sequence in which Caul talks to the girl. Instead, we suddenly get a dream sequence; and before we have fully adjusted to this surprise, the scene is almost over.

When Caul becomes involved in the plot centered on the couple and the Director, so does the audience. The plot, however, is very weak, and this is the next major problem with the film.

Normally, a mystery story moves so rapidly the holes in the plot are obscured, undetected by the audience—at least until after the film ends. But Coppola's repeated inability to deal successfully with his films' pace recurs in *The Conversation*. The pace in this film is very slow. Sometimes, in terms of Caul's character and professional work, the pace must be slow. Nevertheless, dramatically justified or not, the slow pace allows the audience all too much time to ponder the flaws in the script while watching the film.

Would someone as clever and cautious as Caul allow another bugging expert to stick a pen (which does in fact have a bugging device in it) in his jacket pocket without checking the pen out? More important, would Caul, almost paranoid at this point, invite a group of people, including his jealous professional rival, to the warehouse where he had secretly established his office? It is even more unbelievable that, during the party, he would unlock the part of his workshop in which he keeps his private tapes and let everyone walk in and out of it just as he or she pleased. And why would the Director's assistant go to such elaborate lengths to steal Caul's tapes when, having a complete dossier on Caul, the assistant could have arranged to have the tapes stolen any time he wanted to?

Earlier, after refusing to turn over the final tape to the assistant, Caul goes back to the warehouse and only then works until he is able to hear the crucial part of the couple's conversation. Previously, that part was drowned out by the combo's rendition of "Red Red Robin." Why did Caul not solve that sound problem before he delivered the tape the first time? Though the best surveillance man in the business, though paid $15,000 for this tape, he apparently was quite prepared originally to deliver an only partially audible tape of the couple's conversation.

Both the Director and his assistant are veiled in a bit more obscurity than is plausible. Because Caul has been dealing with both men for some time, he must know *something* about them, but the audience is denied even the simplest data. It is not made clear whether the young woman in the park is the Director's wife, daughter, mistress, or upstairs maid. What the assistant is all about is equally unclear. This is perhaps even more annoying because the assistant keeps reappearing in the story. Sometimes he seems to be the Director's loyal right-hand man. Sometimes he seems to be working in cahoots with the couple. At still other times, he seems to be pursuing a third—independent—course.

So, too, at times the assistant seems to need very much to know the information on the tapes. But on other occasions he appears to know already everything about the young couple. This second impression is indicated in the contrived scene in which Caul goes to the Director's office to pick up the money paid him for making the tapes. It is quite unlikely that Caul would be told to pick up his money at a time shortly before the Director is scheduled to meet the couple somewhere else. Furthermore, when Caul enters the office, he is not given the money in an envelope, as he was when the assistant, in an earlier scene, tried to obtain the tapes from Caul. This time the money is all spread out in piles on a desk. Caul must put it all together before leaving. Surely one cannot help suspecting that although both the Director and his assistant want Caul in and out of the office as quickly as possible, the money is spread out because Coppola wants Caul to be in the office for a while.

While present, Caul hears the final tape being played. He also hears the assistant explaining why he obtained the tapes and wanted the Director to hear them. The assistant says to the Director, "I want you to know what you need to know." This statement makes the character of the assistant more confusing than ever. It also makes it appear that Caul previously dealt more with the assistant than the earlier scenes in the film indicated Caul did. None of this qualifies as "rich ambiguity" or a "Kafkaesque complexity." It is just vague and confusing.

The ultimate surprise in the plot is that the innocent-looking couple for whom Caul feels a growing sympathy turn out to be killers, not the victims of killers. It is important that the audience make the same initial assumption that Caul makes. However, because the boy and the girl *are* killers, they must not say or do anything that contradicts this fact. In this context it is hard to accept the bulk of their comments as valid. It is hard to believe that while the couple are firming up their plans to commit murder, they would spend most of their time sympathizing with a panhandler stretched out asleep on a bench. The young woman waxes rhetorical about the fact that the panhandler was once "someone's baby boy." Her partner in crime then talks at even greater length about the sad death of fifty such panhandlers when the newspaper unions went on strike and the panhandlers had no newspapers to keep them warm. The boy also comments, "He's not hurting anyone." The girl replies, "Neither are we." The last comment is surely the phoniest of false leads.

As to the murder itself, it appears that the only reason the Director was stabbed after supposedly having already suffocated to death was to provide the blood needed for Caul to find later. That the murderers, after neatly removing every trace of the murder, would stupidly try to stuff blood-soaked rags down a toilet bowl also seems farfetched. And how did the couple, even if aided by others, manage to remove the body from the hotel? Finally, after repeatedly stabbing the Director until he died, how on earth did the couple manage to make it convincing that the Director died in an auto crash?

The last sequence also strains credulity. It is psychologically plausible that Caul, told his apartment was bugged, would obsessively try to find the hidden microphone by pulling apart the furniture, knocking down the walls, and ripping up the floorboards. It is not plausible that his fellow-tenants, to say nothing of his superintendent, would remain unaware of and indifferent to what he was doing. As photographically and thematically dramatic as is the last scene, in which Caul plays his saxophone in an entirely empty apartment, one cannot help wondering what Caul did with all the furniture.

Other flaws must be cited. Fairly early in the movie, Caul has a "flash-forward" vision of the murder scene. He envisions the dying Director staggering toward the girl in the hotel room, a scene which actually does take place later when the Director is being murdered. It would have been much more plausible if Caul had a vision of the Director murdering the girl—for that is what Caul at the time believes will be the case. Also, the film abruptly shuttles between two styles. A stylistic change in the dream sequence is acceptable. But at other times the style of the photography and of the setting suddenly changes in scenes that are supposed to represent literal reality. For instance, the first time Caul goes to the building where the Director works, the setting is mundanely realistic. Later the same setting is surrealistic.

Apparently Coppola and many of the critics were unaware of a basic problem with regard to Coppola's condemnation of the invasion of privacy instigated by surveillance work. William S. Pechter did spot the problem. He wrote, "To the extent that *The Conversation* is a film about the invasion of privacy, a statement against bugging (and it is only partly this), it's one whose plot could be used (indeed, could more easily be used) to *justify* bugging, in that Harry's surveillance uncovers a plan to commit a murder which thus could conceivably have been prevented."[11]

In pursuing his character delineation of Harry Caul and his convoluted plot, Coppola apparently lost track of all the threads he was trying to weave together. He ended up with a storyline that at least partially contradicted his main thematic premise.

Some of the confusion in *The Conversation* can be traced to one final influence that operated on Coppola while he made the film. Coppola stated, "I think *The Conversation* was very influenced by *Blow-Up*—in that one scene where David Hemmings is blowing up the photograph. It's very similar to the scene in which Hackman goes through the tape. I knew that. It was definitely inspired by or influenced by *Blow-Up*. That one scene."[12]

Actually, the influence of *Blow-Up* is present elsewhere, and usually causes a muddle. For instance, mime figures in *Blow-Up* appear both at the start and at the end of the film, and are of thematic importance. So, too, the very first figure spotlighted in *The Conversation* is a mime figure, who weaves in and out of the crowd in Union Square. Unfortunately, nothing serious—indeed, nothing at all—is made of this figure. He is just there.

A more serious muddle relates to the post-convention party at Caul's workshop and the stealing of his tapes. Coppola based his sequence on similar plot developments in *Blow-Up*, and in so doing caused his sequence to fail. In *Blow-Up*, the Hemmings character, Thomas, a photographer and a swinger, allows himself to become sexually involved with two teen-agers who hang around his studio. So, too, Jane (played by Vanessa Redgrave) walks into the studio without any problem. In sum, it is made quite clear that the photographer's life style is a wide open one. Gaining access to his studio is no problem at all; he practically invites theft. But in *The Conversation* it is repeatedly emphasized that Caul seals off his life from others. He guards his privacy obsessively. It is inconceivable that he would suddenly hold a party in his workshop, open all the locks, and make it so easy for someone to steal his tapes.

Finally, the murder plots in both *Blow-Up* and *The Conversation* are vague. The vagueness in *Blow-Up*, however, is accepted by the audience—for several reasons. The main character, for instance, because he is so caught up in his style of living, is only intermittently interested in the murder plot, and he is easily distracted from pursuing the matter even then. But in *The Conversation* Caul soon comes to care very much about the murder plot. He is also, unlike the photographer in *Blow-Up*, more than a little like a detective. Hence, the viewer is impatient with Caul for finding out so little about the people involved in the murder plot.

Coppola presents an initially very interesting main character in *The Conversation*. Through this character he makes some insightful comments on the contemporary scene. He points out that no matter what they may try to tell themselves, people who deal primarily with techonological equipment, whether they be surveillance men, scientists, or filmmakers, have definite moral responsibilities. He also points out that although modern man has made awesome technological progress, he is still—even with his inventions—pathetically unable to understand the human experience, or himself. Unfortunately, all the flaws in the film outweigh and greatly undermine its good points.

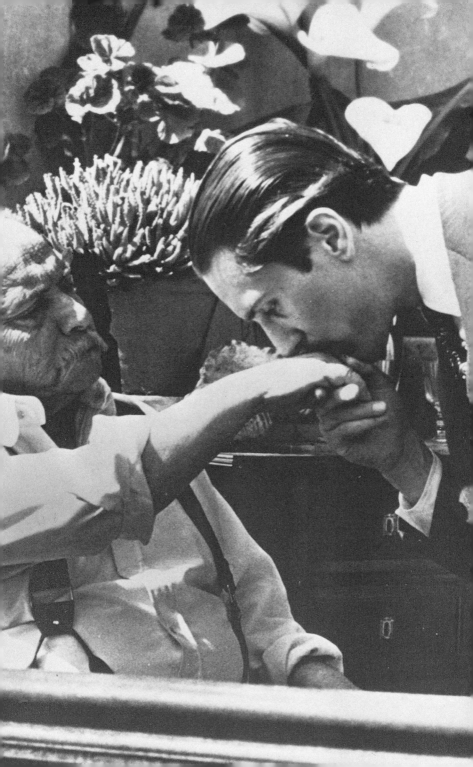

9

"I Began To Be Intrigued"

WHEN WILLIAM MURRAY asked Coppola what led him finally to agree to write and direct a sequel to *The Godfather*, Coppola replied, "Initially, the idea of a sequel seemed horrible to me. It sounded like a tacky spin-off, and I used to joke that the only way I'd do it was if they'd let me film *Abbott and Costello Meet the Godfather*—that would have been fun."

What changed his mind came in an unexpected way. "I entertained some Russian film executives who were visiting San Francisco and they asked me if I was going to make *The Godfather Part II*. That was the first time I heard the phrase used; I guess you could say I stole the title from the Russians."

The Godfather Part II

A streak of the contrary in Coppola also contributed to his decision to attempt a sequel. "It seemed like such a terrible idea that I began to be intrigued by the thought of pulling it off. Simple as that. Sometimes I sit around thinking I'd like to get a job directing a TV soap opera, just to see if I could make it the most wonderful thing of its kind ever done. Or I imagine devoting myself to directing the plays of a cub-scout troop and having it be the most exciting theater in the country. You know that feeling when something seems so outrageous, you just have to do it? That's what happened to me."[1]

But there was more to the situation than this. "I really had made so much money on *The Godfather*, it was irrelevant for me to do a film for any other reason than because I wanted to do it. I didn't like what was then a script called *Death of Michael Corleone*." Coppola realized that what the studio officials were trying to indicate to him "was that they'd let me do anything I wanted. I began to think of

147

letting *The Godfather* format subsidize me in doing something more ambitious in the sequel than they wanted."

Coppola then came up with the idea that spurred him into action. "It was then I made my bargain with them to let me bring back all the original actors that were relevant to my story that I hadn't figured out yet. If it could be a real continuation as though it were really part of the first film and be called *The Godfather,* and if I could have total control over it, I would do it."[2]

Coppola had also been brooding over the failure of the audience to condemn Michael morally as it watched the first *Godfather* film come to its conclusion. He now decided what he would do this second time around concerning his main character. "I wanted to take Michael to what I felt was the logical conclusion. He wins every battle; his brilliance and his resources enable him to defeat all his enemies. I didn't want Michael to die. I didn't want Michael to be put into prison. I didn't want him to be assassinated by his rivals. But, in a bigger sense, I also wanted to destroy Michael. There's no doubt that, by the end of this picture, Michael Corleone, having beaten everyone, is sitting there alone, a living corpse."

In sum, Coppola decided that "Michael Corleone is doomed. There's no way that man is ever going to change. I admit I considered some upbeat touch at the end, like having his son turn against him to indicate he wouldn't follow in that tradition, but honesty— and Pacino—wouldn't let me do it. Michael is doomed."[3]

Coppola wrote the script himself; Puzo made a few significant changes. When Coppola presented the screenplay to Pacino, his leading actor was not completely happy with it. So, Maureen Orth reported, "Coppola rewrote the entire script in three days. Copies for the first actors' reading emerged from the Xerox machine with an hour to spare before filming started. When they read the script, the actors stood and applauded Coppola."[4]

Originally, Coppola assumed that Marlon Brando would participate in the sequel. But Brando and the management at Paramount had a falling out. Coppola soon realized that there was no chance that Brando would be a part of the sequel. At first, Coppola was keenly disappointed. But, as he commented later, "When I got into working with Bob DeNiro, obviously it meant that he could play the character much younger, which is what I had wanted. I think it worked out really well."[5]

Coppola also gave more thought to the character of Kay. Com-

menting on the length of time that passes before the marriage between Kay and Michael begins to plummet, he said later, "It may
seem like a long time, but actually they're together only six or seven
years. How many people do we know who stay together unhappily
for 15 years or more before they finally split? Also, during the
Fifties, there were a lot of forces that tended to keep men and
women together way beyond the point when they should have
parted. Think of how many husbands have kept their wives and held
their families together by promising that things would change just as
soon as they became vice-presidents or had $100,000 in the bank or
closed the big deal. I've strung my own wife along for 13 years by
telling her that as soon as I was done with this or that project, I'd
stop working so hard and we'd live a more normal life. I mean, that's
the classic way husbands lie . . . . Michael lies to Kay in that way and
she believes him at first—because she wants to believe him."

Coppola went on to say that it was not only Kay who wanted to
believe the lies. It was also Michael. To illustrate his point, Coppola
spoke about his own profession. "People like myself, who decide
that it's necessary to work within a system in order to be able either
to change it or eventually to go off on their own to subsidize the kind
of work they believe in, inevitably become changed by the process,
if they go along with it. I know a lot of bright young writers and
directors in Hollywood who are very successful—some of them I
gave jobs to four and five years ago—and they're making a lot of
money; but they're no longer talking about the things they used to
talk about. Their conversation now is all about deals, about what's
going to sell and what isn't. And they rave about their new cars and
their new $400,000 houses. They don't even see or hear the changes
in themselves. They've become the very people they were criticiz-
ing three years ago. Like Michael, they've become their fathers
. . . . One of the reasons I live here [in San Francisco] and not in
Los Angeles is that I'm trying to keep my bearings."[6]

Although he was given a huge budget for the sequel, Coppola was
by no means free of worry. He was simply placed in a different kind
of pressure-packed situation. He knew, for instance, that the sequel
would have to earn approximately twenty-five million dollars to
clear expenses. This prompted him to describe his professional work
in terms that have since become famous. "You know what it's like to
be a director?" he said. "It's like running in front of a locomotive. If
you stop, if you trip, if you make a mistake, you get killed. How can

you be creative with that thing behind you? Every day I know it's $8,000 an hour. It forces me into decisions I know will work."[7]

Coppola shot the film in a variety of locations, including Lake Tahoe, Las Vegas, Washington, Sicily, and the Dominican Republic. While he worked in Santo Domingo, it rained day after day. But a still bigger problem was Al Pacino's health. Pacino reached the point of exhaustion. Coppola told Murray, "The role of Michael is a very strange and difficult one and it put a terrific strain on [Pacino]. It was like being caught in a kind of vise. In the first picture, he went from being a young, slightly insecure, naive and brilliant young college student to becoming this horrible Mafia killer. In *Godfather II*, he's the same man from beginning to end—working on a much more subtle level, very rarely having a big climactic scene where an actor can unload . . . . The entire performance had to be kind of vague and so understated that, as an actor, you couldn't really be sure what you were doing. You had the tremendous pressure of not knowing whether you were creating a monster or just being terrible. The load on Al was terrific and it really ran him down physically."

After nine months, the principal photography had been completed. The problem of editing the film, however, had just begun. Coppola revealed to Murray that whole sections concerning the rise of young Vito Corleone had to be deleted from the movie, which was running far too long. "My heart was really in the Little Italy sequences," Coppola remarked afterward, "in the old streets of New York, the music, all that turn-of-the-century atmosphere. I had great scenes in the script that we couldn't include in the movie: There was one where Enrico Caruso showed up in the neighborhood and sang *Over There* to get guys to enlist for World War One; I had scenes of Italians building the subways, of young Vito courting his girl and joining his friends for music and mandolins and wine."[8]

In the weeks preceding the world première at Christmas time, 1974, the work on editing the film continued relentlessly. Yet, at a sneak preview in San Diego, Coppola still felt that the film was in trouble. As *Time* reported it, the last hour of the film "seemed jumbled, confused, cold. All during the showing Coppola muttered notes to himself into a pocket tape recorder. Some scenes needed lengthening, others were dropped. The idea of an intermission was scrapped."

Back in San Francisco, Coppola had to complete the final

editing—editing that needed weeks' worth of time and effort—in a matter of days. At one point, Coppola snapped, "Never, never, never again will I work under such chaotic conditions. If I had three more months on this one, I'd have a great film."[9] Nonetheless, the task was finished.

There are two main plotlines in *The Godfather, Part II*. After an opening shot, a close-up of Michael's face, the first plot begins to unfold. This plot presents the early life of Michael's father, Vito Corleone. It starts with a funeral procession. Vito's father, who opposed the Mafia in his Sicilian town and was murdered, is being carried to the cemetery. Soon the Mafia chief kills both Vito's brother and his mother. Vito is smuggled out of town and out of the country. At Ellis Island he is quarantined.

The film switches to the party celebrating the First Communion of Michael's son. At the party, Senator Geary refuses to help Michael obtain a gambling license; Johnny Ola, a Hyman Roth henchman, and Michael discuss the possibility of a meeting between Roth and Michael; and Michael's sister Connie tells him she wants to remarry. Frankie Pentangeli reports that he is having trouble in New York with Roth's men—but Michael offers him no help. Still later, Michael's wife, Kay, tells him she is pregnant and is unhappy because Michael has not kept his promise to phase out all his illegitimate business activities. That night, while Michael and Kay are in their bedroom, an attempt is made on Michael's life.

Now the film switches back to Vito Corleone. Vito is working for a grocer in the Little Italy section of New York. One evening he attends a local theater and sees Fanucci, a gangster from the neighborhood. On another evening he agrees to hide some revolvers belonging to other gangsters. Later they reward him with a stolen rug. He loses his job because the grocer is forced to hire Fanucci's relative in Vito's place.

In the next segment Michael meets with Roth, who appears cooperative. Michael tells Frankie to let Roth's men have their way for the time being. Johnny Ola learns from Michael's brother Freddie that Frankie will meet with Roth's men alone. At the meeting Frankie is almost killed—and is told that Michael betrayed him. Meanwhile, Senator Geary is tricked into believing that he murdered a prostitute. In return for Michael's protection, Geary will get Michael a license.

Because of the schemes aimed at Michael, Kay is confined to her home for her own safety. This intensifies her unhappiness with her marriage. Michael flies to Cuba to meet with Roth and with corrupt Cuban government officials. During one night's entertainment Michael discovers that Freddie helped Roth attempt to kill Michael. Michael's right-hand man kills Ola, but, during the upheaval of a revolution, fails to kill Roth. When he returns to the United States, Michael learns that Kay had a miscarriage and their baby boy is dead.

Now the switches between the two life stories move more rapidly. First, we learn that Vito has joined the gang that asked him to hide the revolvers. When Fanucci demands a percentage of the gang's take, Vito kills him. Next, Michael returns home. But Kay and himself have nothing to say to each other. Then, Vito convinces a local landlord to be kinder to a tenant, an old lady who sought Vito's aid.

A longer sequence revolves around a senate investigating committee's attempt to put Michael in prison. Frankie, still thinking that Michael double-crossed him, at first cooperates with the committee. But when his older brother remains loyal to Michael, Frankie decides to do the same. Later, prompted by Michael's questions, Freddie explains that he betrayed Michael because he resented being Michael's errand boy year after year. Kay tells Michael that she wants to take their children and leave Michael. When he protests, she tells him that she did not have a miscarriage, she had an abortion. Furious, Michael tells her that she can leave, but she cannot have the children.

In the next flashback, Vito and his family return to Sicily for a visit. Here, Vito stabs to death the old Mafia chief who killed his parents and his brother. Back in the present, Michael, Connie, and Freddie meet at the funeral service for their mother. Connie—her personal life a mess—promises to take care of Michael and begs him to forgive Freddie. But Michael proves cold. He also rejects Kay's plea for forgiveness. He pressures Frankie into committing suicide. And he has both Freddie and Roth shot.

Then, a flashback of a different kind takes place. The Japanese have attacked Pearl Harbor, and the Corleone offspring are waiting for their father to come home. Michael tells the others he has enlisted because he wants to determine his own future. Angry at Michael, all of the others run out of the room to greet the Don. Michael is left alone.

The film ends with two quick shots. One is of Vito leaving Sicily with his family. The other is of Michael brooding after Freddie is killed.

Analysis

The Godfather, Part II does succeed in being more than another good gangster film. It is a richer, though not a more exciting film than *The Godfather*.

Yet it has its flaws. For instance, the first major sequence, describing Vito's boyhood in Sicily, begins with a funeral procession in which the body of Vito's father is carried toward a graveyard. There is a very quick succession of scenes. The procession is halted almost immediately by the shotgun-killing of Vito's older brother. Then Vito's mother, taking little Vito with her, begs the local Mafia chief to allow Vito to live; when her plea is spurned, she (implausibly) attacks the chief right then and there and is killed. Vito (implausibly) outruns all the pursuing bodyguards. Then he flees from the town. All of these events occur so rapidly they cannot be reacted to sensitively. They are merely bad melodrama.

The characterization of Senator Geary constitutes another serious flaw. Coppola overdoes the trick of making Michael and his family and his friends appear attractive by making Michael's enemies thoroughly unattractive. Geary is made one hundred and ten per cent rotten. He is hypocritical, conniving, heartless, perverted, viciously prejudiced, foul-mouthed. At the Communion celebration, right in front of Michael and his bodyguards, Geary refers sneeringly to Michael's "fucking family." And that is the least nasty thing he says. In his later appearances, he is never one iota less despicable. It is just too much.

In the early sequence, to emphasize Michael's superiority to Geary, Coppola makes Michael slip out of character. That Michael would tell Geary no payoff money will be given in order to obtain a gambling license is quite possible and in character. That Michael would then predict that Geary will end up paying the license fee himself is not in character. Michael would never tip his hand this way. (It should also be noted that Geary does not take the warning at all seriously. Could such a powerful, cunning politician be *that* stupid?)

The script and the editing do not make it clear whether the

attempted assassination of Frankie Pentangeli is successful or not.
The Cuban sequence is even weaker. Michael confides in Freddie,
telling him about a forthcoming plot on Michael's life. No such plot
unfolds, however. Instead, we are given some Cecil B. DeMille-like
spectacles. At the first one Michael learns that Freddie betrayed
him—but this intensely dramatic moment is smothered by the
spectacle.

During another spectacle, a New Year's Eve party, various
groups of unidentified troops march here and there. For some reason, troops march into the hospital room occupied by Roth. They
arrive just in time to kill one of Michael's men, who was in the
process of murdering Roth. Once more, we have no clear idea
whether the murder attempt was successful or not. When Michael
tells Freddie that he knows Freddie double-crossed him, Freddie
literally backs away from Michael. Yet, later, he resumes living in
Michael's compound. All of this is confusing and annoying.

The pace of Vito's rise to prominence in Little Italy is at first a bit
too slow. Then it speeds up too much. At one point, Vito tries in
vain to convince a landlord to be kind to a tenant. In the very next
scene, the same landlord enters Vito's store and fawns all over him.
In Puzo's novel, it is made clear that, in the interim, the landlord
found out about Vito's already-intimidating reputation. In the
movie, what caused the complete about-face is not dramatized.

Vito's return to Sicily is overlong. But its worst flaw is the blatant
impossibility of Vito's remarkably easy killing of the old Mafia chief.
Though a stranger, though holding a coat (on a very hot day) over his
arm—and clutching a butcher knife under the coat, Vito is permitted to walk right up to the chief. After he cuts up the chief, he easily
escapes, even though he is deep inside the chief's grounds and
surrounded by the chief's henchmen. Most implausible of all, no
attempt at retaliation takes place during the rest of Vito's stay in
town. As Stanley Kauffmann points out, at the end of this sequence
Vito and his family gaily board a train to start the trek home right in
the middle of a town thickly populated with the murdered Mafia
chief's henchmen.[10]

Nonetheless, the film's virtues decisively outweigh its flaws.
Every sequence, even the weakest, rewards the viewer for his at-
tentiveness. The film grippingly dramatizes how, step by step, the
murder of Michael's grandfather, a murder committed by a local
band of Mafia men in a town in Sicily long before Michael was born,

led to Michael's sitting alone in his Lake Tahoe estate and brooding about the loss of so much of his family—the family that was the *raison d'être* for all the major actions undertaken by the Corleones.

Beginning with that first Sicilian sequence, the film also dramatizes the code that demands revenge for a wrong done to a family. Vito's older brother is killed because he seeks to avenge his father's death. Vito's mother understands that Vito, too, will be killed; and she dies in an attempt both to avenge and to protect. And Vito, finally, avenges all these murders.

The desire for revenge explains most of the Mafia murders in the first *Godfather* film too. It explains Michael's entrance into the family "business." It explains why, in *Part II*, Michael feels he must shed so much blood, including the blood of his only remaining brother. As Pauline Kael wrote, Michael "chose to become a killer out of family loyalty." He "can never go back to the time before that moment in the restaurant when he shot his father's enemies."[11] Coppola himself tried to steer the audience to this primary theme in the film. Just before the film was released, he stated what the major point of his plot was. "I want to show how two men, father and son, were . . . corrupted by this Sicilian waltz of vengeance."[12]

The murder of Michael's grandfather seems to lead relentlessly to Michael's ultimate isolation because the code of revenge is so deterministic. The film shows how a man such as Michael can become locked into a life consisting of seeking revenge for wrongs done to him and his family and then being on guard against retaliations—retaliations which, if instigated, must in turn be retaliated against. Michael also knows that the Corleones' enemies would consider failure to seek revenge a sign of weakness, and that this would encourage those enemies to attack again; for the world of the Sicilian peasant and of the American gangster is a stark, primitive world.

Yet what Michael gradually comes to perceive is that constantly destroying your enemies is ultimately self-destructive. Thus, he ends up all-powerful, but totally unable to alter his empty life.

There is, then, a special poignancy in the scene in which young Vito is quarantined on Ellis Island. He sits on a chair that is so big for him he can swing his legs back and forth. He gazes out the window and sings—the first time he utters a sound in the movie. His singing is so replete with innocence and happiness. Yet, although Vito has escaped from Sicily, he has not escaped from violence.

Except for the characterization of Geary, the day highlighted by Michael's party for his son is excellent. The sight of Michael's men perched with rifles on the roofs surrounding the festivities succinctly points to the price that must be paid for the power funding the party. Equally significant, the party is in celebration of a First Communion. Religion and gangsterism are juxtaposed many times. Several religious ceremonies were pictured or alluded to in the first *Godfather* film. It began with a wedding celebration and concluded with a baptism. More religious ceremonies are referred to in *Part II*.

In this way it is made abundantly clear that, at least for many of the males in the Mafia, religion, like so much else in their lives, is primarily a matter of rituals adhered to at the prescribed intervals. They are conservatives; their parasitical "business" schemes depend on everything remaining unchanged. Unsettled and angered by change, they very much prefer that everything—including such a fundamental matter as religion—be the way it was when they grew to manhood. Respect is shown and money is given to the Church. Religion is a definite part of one's private life. It is especially helpful in training female members of the family to be decent and dutiful.

But religion is in no way allowed to interfere with one's "business" activities. It is, without conscious effort, subsumed by these activities. Though it is always present in his environment, it provides no source of strength for Michael, for he gives it no serious thought. It does not shape him, or save him.

Unlike the situation when Connie first wed, here at the Communion celebration, troubles and unhappiness are not peripheral; they are central. Michael's sister is so self-centered that she has to be reminded by her mother to go see her own children before she tries to speak to Michael about what she wants. When she presents her lover to Michael, it is obvious that the man is worthless. Freddie proves unable to handle his wife, who gets drunk and makes a scene. This is an early indication that Freddie has marital and personality problems, problems that goad him into betraying Michael.

Further proof that the party's gaiety is mostly illusory is given by the presence of Johnny Ola, representing Hyman Roth. Ola stresses that Roth wants only to cooperate with Michael, but before the night is over, Roth's men will attempt to murder Michael. Frankie Pentangeli complains of trouble in his New York domain. Here Michael blunders. He is after such "big game" he cannot fully explain his scheme even to a loyalist such as Frankie. His cryptic comments (as well as his sophisticated life style) fail to reassure Frankie, a mistake that almost causes Frankie, first, to help send Michael to jail, and eventually costs Frankie his life.

Geary refuses to aid Michael (whereas Don Vito Corleone did gain the willing cooperation of his political contemporaries). On this same day, Kay tells Michael of her bitter disappointment that, despite his promises, he has not rid himself of all illegal operations by this seventh year of their marriage. Finally, there is the hair-raising scene in their bedroom. Kay happens to wonder aloud why on this night the bedroom drapes are still open. His mind instantly accelerating to high speed, Michael intuits an assassination attempt and manages to pull Kay down onto the floor beside him just a moment before a hail of bullets rips the room apart. It could not be clearer that although Michael has already gained more wealth and power than his father ever obtained, this fabulous gain has been won at a price Michael has only begun to pay.

The difference between appearance and reality permeates the next sequence, too. Vito is supposedly free of violence and gangs, both of which thrived in Sicily. But as he sits down to enjoy an "opera" offered in Little Italy, he is reminded that violence thrives in this environment. The gangster Fanucci is permitted to disrupt the performance as he leaves. After the show, Vito sees Fanucci threaten the life of the theater owner's daughter in his successful attempt to extort more money from the owner. Vito learns more about violence in the New World when he is asked to hide several revolvers, when he is fired because Fanucci insists his relative be given Vito's job, and when, to reward him for hiding the guns, gangsters steal an expensive rug for him—and almost shoot a policeman in the process.

Vito accepts the rug, and this is a turning point in his life. Symbolically, he is accepting the proposition that violence is the key to improving one's lot in life. Vito's son Michael will also accept this belief.

In the next sequence, Michael meets with Roth in Florida and, eager for Roth to underestimate his intelligence, declares that he knows the assassination attempt was not the work of Roth. He meets next with Frankie and tells him to give way to the pressure of Roth's cohorts in New York. What is emphasized here is the deviousness not just of the Corleone family's enemies, but of Michael too. Vito Corleone, in *Part I*, never asked his men to do what Michael asks

Frankie to do: to lie down and take it from outsiders in order that the family might eventually triumph. This is precisely why the misunderstanding between Michael and Frankie grows. Frankie, an old-timer, knows only the code and methods by which Vito Corleone ran the family. More deviousness and violence occur when, to bring Geary to his knees, a prostitute is killed and Geary is tricked into believing he did it.

Later, in Cuba, while talking with Roth, Michael indicates that he knows Roth's men tried to kill Frankie. Roth does not bat an eye. Instead, he lectures Michael, telling him to let nothing interfere with profit. This stresses another motif. Right after the attempt on Michael's life, Michael spoke with Tom about what holds private families and "families" of criminals together. Usually, it is financial gain. Michael believes that his two families are held together primarily by something better—loyalty.

As brilliant as he is, then, Michael is living under an illusion to some degree. For, while still in Cuba, he learns that the insider who helped make the attempt on his life possible was his brother Freddie. Back in the States, he is told that Kay has lost the baby she was carrying; he will eventually learn from Kay herself that she had the baby killed.

In the next flashback, Vito tricks and murders Fanucci during a religious street-ritual. To cover his tracks, Vito quickly returns to where his family sits watching the ceremony. Here, in contrast to what is happening in Michael's family circle, love and closeness permeate the scene. John Yates remarked on this particular emphasis on family. "The scene switches back and forth repeatedly from a family scene in Vito's young manhood to a family scene in Michael's time. Michael gazes at his sleeping son before he leaves Tahoe for Miami, and the scene fades to Vito, in a 1918 tenement, gazing at his first son in the same ancient way. Michael returns to Tahoe, demanding to know if his aborted fetus was a son, and again we see Vito watching, as the infant Fredo is treated for pneumonia. Vito returns from the murder of Fanucci to his family stoop, saying, 'Michael, your father loves you very much;' and in the next scene an adult Michael returns to a frigid home, his son's toy car buried in the snow, his wife sewing in an empty room."[13]

In the sequence that begins with Michael's moving past the snow-covered toy car, we learn that Michael has become increasingly fearful that his every triumph is costing him more than whatever it is he wins. He asks his mother if a man who tries to be "strong for his family" can nonetheless "lose" his family. His mother, when she thinks she finally understands the question, reassures Michael that a person can never lose his family. But Michael is not reassured. And, as later events show, his uneasiness is all too clearly proven justified.

The next two sequences, for example, spotlight quite different stages in the careers of Vito and his son Michael. Vito is seen as someone who is already trying to move beyond the sphere of crime. He opens a legitimate business and proudly watches as the store sign is hoisted above the front door. He is also becoming a Godfather-figure in the best sense of the term. He helps an old lady with her landlord.

On the other hand, while Vito's private world is expanding, Michael's private world is shrinking. Frankie Pentangeli almost does Michael in at the senate investigation. Michael successfully utilizes the Sicilian stress on loyalty by bringing Frankie's brother to the senate proceedings in order to urge Frankie not to turn informer. But Michael cannot thereby spark more warmth and love in the world he now lives in.

The next scene—perhaps the single most emotionally powerful scene in either *Godfather* film—features the climactic confrontation between Michael and his wife Kay. While their children, innocent and bored, wait outside the hotel suite, Kay congratulates Michael on once again outmaneuvering his enemies (this time, the senate investigating committee). Then she tells him she wants to take the children and leave him. Michael once more promises to shed all his illegal business operations. But Kay knows now that Michael will never do so, never willingly give up any part of his awesome power, never—later in life—retire and, like his father, grow vegetables in the backyard and play the buffoon for the entertainment of his grandson. She tells him that she no longer feels any love for him— the starkest comment made by anyone on the emptiness in Michael's life.

Dropping his mask of tolerance and, in so doing, proving how really cold he has become, Michael tells Kay he would never let his children go from him. It is at this moment that Kay declares she did not have a miscarriage, she had an abortion.

It is a stunning moment.

Michael, who is so enormously skillful at evading blows aimed at him, and who is so enormously skillful at disguising what he is really thinking and feeling, is visibly staggered by this blow. Trembling with mounting rage, he slaps Kay across the face. Yet it is she who has delivered, by far, the worse blow.

All Michael can think to do now is banish Kay from his life, thus shrinking his family and his emotional life still more.

Now, acts of vengeance dominate. Once again the present is closely juxtaposed with the past. Though implausible, Vito's knifing of the old Mafia chieftain is a powerful scene. The initial quietness of the scene (a quietness emphasized by the chief's sleepiness and soft mutterings) and then the sudden thrust of the knife and the rapid retreat—all are masterfully dramatized. The scene is thematically powerful, too. For in this early moment in the lives of the Corleone family, the situation is relatively simple. Despite the brutality of the murder, the audience feels a sense of satisfaction. A long-awaited retaliation has taken place against a foe who deserved what he got.

But the parallel series of deaths that Michael instigates are not all that simple. The murder of Roth is somewhat similar in context to the murder of the Mafia chief. The other two deaths, however, are only depressing. Frankie must commit suicide because he is trapped in a dead-end situation, the sad result of misunderstandings and blunders on his part and, even more, on Michael's part. If Michael had made his scheme clear to Frankie, if Michael's scheme had been less complicated, and if Frankie, in his turn, had not let himself be hoodwinked by Roth's men, Frankie would never have become trapped in such a situation.

To make the whole matter even more dismal, there is more than a little sad irony in the fact that Tom Hagen, the longtime friend of the Corleone family, is the one who reassures Frankie that, after his death, his people will be taken care of. For the movie has also shown that whatever closeness of feeling existed in the past between Tom and Michael, there is none now. Tom is not consulted about most of the Corleones' operations any more. When he is trying to tell Michael about the death of the baby Kay was carrying, Tom, in attempting to handle the matter as delicately as he can in order to spare Michael's feelings, only incurs the wrath of Michael, who lashes out at him. But the biggest insult of all occurs when Michael talks with Tom about his plans to kill Roth and reaffirm his position of power. Michael asks Tom how far he will support him. The lack of trust Michael has in Tom stings Tom savagely. Tom cannot refrain from telling Michael how terribly hurt he feels because Michael asked him such a question.

Yet Frankie's death and the deterioration of the friendship between Tom and Michael, however sad, are still not nearly as depressing as the death of Michael's brother Freddie. The scene in which Freddie explains to Michael how he let himself be suckered into becoming the tool of Roth is a quiet, thoroughly moving scene. Filled with anger, bitterness, and anguish, Freddie reveals the years and years of frustration that gnawed at him as he watched his "kid brother" move into a position of power within the family organization and increase that power while he, an older brother, went nowhere. Unwilling to admit his own mediocrity, he can only fumblingly articulate the fierce resentment he felt at being relegated to little more than an errand boy. He blurts out his pathetic desire to do something on his own, something not set up for him by his "kid brother." It becomes painfully clear how Freddie allowed himself to be duped by Roth.

In *Part I*, the worst thing Michael had to contemplate doing was killing his wastrel brother-in-law after the latter helped arrange the murder of Sonny. It was not, finally, a difficult decision to make. The potential victim was contemptible. Freddie is no such thing. He is a weak, confused, spiteful fool. According to the code Michael lives by, however, Freddie must be killed. So, while he sits fishing in a rowboat and recites a prayer (a "trick" he used to play on his brothers in order—quite typically—to be one up on them by catching more fish than they did), Freddie is shot in the back of the head by Michael's top gunman.

While these deaths take place, Michael sits in deep shadows. Vito, a youngster quarantined on Ellis Island, sat on a big chair and sang. Michael sits in a big chair as if he were a king on a throne. But he is an emotionally empty king, and almost all alone. There is little left of his family. His mother and father are dead. Sonny has been gunned down. Michael has had his other brother, Freddie, and his brother-in-law killed. His first wife was murdered by his enemies. And his second wife visits her children only when Michael is out of sight. One such time, Kay—lonely and full of regrets—stands just outside an open door when Michael comes home. She looks directly at Michael, and her eyes plead for compassion and understanding. Michael shuts the door in her face.

Besides the still-young children, who rarely see their father, the only one left is his sister Connie. But Connie is burned out. All of her relations with men have ended dismally. She has nothing now except Michael. She admits to Michael that she sought the kind of men she did because she was rebelling against Michael's power, a motive that echoes Freddie's. She pleads with Michael on behalf of her male counterpart, Freddie. So, the movie begins with a woman begging a man to spare her son. As the movie draws to an end, another woman begs another man to spare their brother. Both pleas are spurned; vengeance must be served.

The last major flashback, to a time shortly after Pearl Harbor was bombed, is richly provocative. While Michael, Sonny, Tom, and the rest of the family wait for the Don to come home, Michael announces that he has enlisted in the armed forces. Several things are in play here. To some degree, Michael at this point in his life is at least somewhat idealistic. His narrow obsession about his family—an obsession that will cost outsiders, members of the family, and himself so much—has yet to awaken. He is also, like his brothers and sister, rebellious, but, unlike them, he is self-reliant. Thus, it is also beyond dispute that Michael, a strong-minded, willful individual, *chooses* to lead the life he in fact leads. Michael is abused and shunned in this scene because he chooses to act outside the best interests and the wishes of the family.

In the short penultimate scene in the movie, Vito is seen leaving Sicily the second time. As the train pulls away, he holds his baby son Michael. Vito has been thoroughly successful in avenging the deaths of his parents and his brother, and in nurturing the prosperity of the family he fathers. But he has also created a complex situation that will result ultimately in the dissolution of his family. In the final scene, we again see Michael brooding as he sits in the shadows. Now, ironically, he is alone not because he chose to act outside the interests of the family, but because he has relentlessly acted in the best interests of the family, and of himself.

It is a fitting ending to a fine movie.

Finally, there is the matter of the acting. The quality of the performances ranges from competent to superb. The characters used almost solely to forward the plot did not offer the actors playing those characters all that much to work with. Such performers as Robert Duvall (Tom), Talia Shire (Connie), and even Michael V. Gazzo (Frankie) were often on and off the screen so quickly there was little they could do to develop their roles. Nonetheless, Duvall brought to bear exactly the right combination of hurt feelings and dignity in the scene where Michael crudely asks Tom if the latter will continue to support him. When Connie returns to Michael's compound to live, Talia Shire kept Connie's confession and plea from becoming embarrassingly sentimental. And Gazzo did well enough at the Communion party when Frankie felt out of place amid the sophisticated surroundings.

However, Gazzo and, in bigger roles, Lee Strasberg (Roth) and Robert DeNiro (Vito Corleone) were not wholly successful. They failed to vary their characterizations very much. Gazzo played one note of bewilderment over and over. At other times, he just seemed self-conscious. Because Roth was so often angry, and therefore spitting out words (such as when he talks about Moe Greene), Strasberg's staccato monotone was frequently apropos. Nonetheless, it became monotonous and dull. Strasberg was most interesting in his last scene when he returns to the United States. Here, he—and the script—allowed Roth more variety of mood. DeNiro, as competent as he was in his part, rarely indicated the underside of Vito Corleone. DeNiro conveyed Vito's deceptively simple—almost simpleminded—exterior. But, except when Vito was actually killing somebody, DeNiro failed to convey Vito's cunning and intelligence, coldness and strength.

Diane Keaton (Kay), John Cazale (Freddie), and Al Pacino (Michael), on the other hand, were excellent. Keaton gave us a complex, intensely alive Kay who was sometimes smoothly able to perform her various roles as wife and mother even when her heart was not in those roles; who was sometimes weary or bitter, sometimes unable—despite what she knew—to stop rooting for her husband to outwit his opponents; sometimes brutally cold, sometimes churning inside, sometimes frustrated and furious, sometimes desperately fighting for Michael's love and for the happiness of her family, sometimes sure of herself, and sometimes confused, regretful, and pleading for compassion. Cazale took on a role that could have been a one-dimensional, whining bore and made Freddie a person we come to care about very much. Cazale presented the complicated mixture of pain and anger, frustration and nastiness, bewilderment and stupidity embodied in Freddie. His Freddie ends up exasperating us because we come to realize that Michael's punishment of Freddie is both just and—somehow—wrong.

Pacino, in an extremely difficult, draining role, is superb. His role is mostly low-key. Yet, unlike DeNiro, Pacino *is* able to imply the often-camouflaged underside of his character. Michael appears to be cool and always in control. The mask he wears is almost always expressionless. Yet one never doubts or forgets that there is great power and determination beneath that exterior. Note, for instance, the moment at Mrs. Corleone's funeral when Michael, after listening to Connie's plea on behalf of Freddie, embraces Freddie. One wonders whether Michael will, in fact, forgive his brother or whether he will have him killed. Then Michael looks over Freddie's shoulder at a henchman; Pacino, though silent, makes it clear what Michael's answer to that question is.

Yet when Pacino wants to erupt, to let it all out, he is even more impressive. If, in the confrontation between Kay and Michael, Keaton is excellent, Pacino is overwhelming. No one could see Pacino's face when Kay tells Michael she had an abortion and not be totally enthralled by the shock and slowly mounting rage expressed in that face.

10

"The Beginning, The Middle, And The End"

Various Ventures

THE MAKING OF *The Conversation* and *The Godfather, Part II* were the two major projects Coppola worked on immediately following the enormous success of the original *Godfather* film. Two other important projects he focused his energy on were George Lucas' *American Graffiti* and the formation of the Directors Company. But he was a part of other undertakings as well.

He was a central figure in the announced television plans pertaining to both *Godfather* films. NBC bought the television rights to the films. The original *Godfather* film, edited by Coppola, was shown once—to an estimated ninety million viewers. Another part of the plan called for a presentation of all the footage in both *Godfather* films, plus much of the footage cut from the two movies before they were released to movie audiences.

Newsweek reported that "Coppola is especially pleased at the prospect of restoring segments—so far unselected—that he had deleted because they ran too long or didn't advance the films' narrative. 'The things that always go are the things you like best but can't justify,' he says. 'Some of the scenes we cut out I just cry about.' Coppola is more than willing to risk tampering with the success of the 'Godfathers' for the television project. . . . 'I promise we will set it ambitiously. There's a 10 per cent chance we'll fail.' "[1]

Coppola also began to reorganize the old American Zoetrope operation into the Coppola Company, a multimedia enterprise. He acquired almost ten per cent of Cinema 5, a film distribution company that owned almost a dozen Manhattan theaters. He encouraged Carroll Ballard, a friend from graduate-school days, to rewrite

Gene Hackman (Harry Caul) in The Conversation
Credit: The Museum of Modern Art/Film Stills Archive

his screenplay *The Black Stallion* and promised to finance the filming of the script. And he bankrolled a magazine, *City of San Francisco*, which was already in operation.

When Coppola took over the running of the magazine, he was—as usual—quite enthusiastic and optimistic. According to *Newsweek*, "The first revamped issue of *City*, dated July 6 [1975], switched to a splashy tabloid format chock-a-block with trendy insights into local culture. Coppola followed through on a promise to chop away at 'cosmopolitan baloney' with a sneering critique of the Bay Area's overzealous vice squad (according to the article, the squad had arrested some aged pensioners for playing penny-ante poker)."

Coppola stated in his magazine that there would be a series of guest editors who would make the periodical even livelier. Warren Hinckle's issue "include a paean to the sensuousness of foot massage, a psycho-portrait of Jack London and his 'macho' obsession, the confessions of a CIA 'contact pilot,' and an attack on SDS founder Tom Hayden." On the cover was "an irate, scantily clad wench pointedly ignored by two gentlemen on barstools, with the headline WHY WOMEN CAN'T GET LAID IN SAN FRANCISCO." *Newsweek* added, "Although Coppola himself confesses to finding the article 'a little sensational for my tastes,' it made his magazine the outraged talk of San Francisco—and helped put Hinckle on the payroll."[2]

As permanent editor, Hinckle never succeeded in selling enough copies of an issue to show a profit. Losses continued to mount. Busy with other projects and more than a little desperate, Coppola brought in his wife Eleanor to "oversee" production. Actually, her primary responsibility was to check on what Hinckle was doing, or not doing. The new arrangement did not do any good. Coppola closed down the magazine. He had lost, news reports estimated, approximately $1,500,000.

Despite her foray into the magazine world, Eleanor was on the whole more than content to remain far from the spotlight which now never seemed to forsake her husband. Coppola remarked, "My wife is a very private person, which is probably why I'm still married to her, because I'm a big consumer of things and people, but I know I can't consume her, so I could never get tired of her." Elaborating, he said, "The best definition I can give you of my wife is that she's an impossible person to buy a present for, because there's nothing she wants. You know what I once gave her for Christmas? The kids were opening their presents and I went into the other room and made her a cappuccino, put it in a box, wrapped it up, brought it out and gave it to her. To this day, she maintains it's the best present she ever got, because she really wanted that cup of coffee. That's the way she is."[3]

At this point in his life, Coppola and his wife and their three children, Gian-Carlo, Roman, and Sophia, lived in a twenty-eight-room house in San Francisco. When interviewed at home or elsewhere, Coppola spoke of various ideas he had for movie projects. One idea centered on an all-girl band. Another plot featured twins who were physically identical, but whose characters were antipodal. The twins would be a boy and girl, and he would use them as a means of "exploring the male-female duality in every individual."[4] Still another idea stemmed from Coppola's lifelong interest in gadgets and machines, especially the automobile—a fitting preoccupation for someone born in Detroit. (Coppola's middle name is the result of his having been born in the Henry Ford Hospital.) He frequently expressed his desire to make a movie based on the life of Preston Tucker, who had worked on important auto inventions, but who was never able to manufacture a car that incorporated his ideas.

Coppola spoke at length about Tucker in relation to the American culture. "Traditionally, our greatest heroes have been creators and inventors. A hundred years ago, what we paraded before the world was something called Yankee ingenuity. Every one of our great cartels and corporations was started by—that is, the original impulse came from—an Andrew Carnegie or a Thomas Edison or a Henry Ford, guys who used their inventive genius to create something better. . . . By the Forties, after the United States had demonstrated that the ultimate result of this ingenuity was our emergence as the most powerful nation in the world, we were being run by huge, entrenched institutions completely hostile to that kind of inventiveness. By 1941, Henry Ford couldn't have built his cheap car. We might have *had* a Henry Ford in the Forties. His name was Preston Tucker."

Coppola elaborated on what he thought Tucker stood for. "Tucker designed a car that could be built for a fraction of the kind of money the major companies were spending on their new models. It was a safe car, a revolutionary car in terms of engineering, and it was a beautiful car. In every way, it was a much better machine than the stuff the major companies were offering, the companies created by Ford and the others. But Tucker was called a fraud and he was destroyed. . . . I'm going to make a film of Tucker's story some-day."[5]

Yet, curiously enough, on another occasion Coppola spoke of Tucker from a quite different perspective. "I like him because he feels human, the lovable American con man, the used-car salesman with his heart in the right place. In his way he was a charlatan. He wore those brown and white pointy shoes, and he was handsome and good with the ladies. He talked fast. He was a little stinky. Some people say I identify with him because he was a con man who was talented. Do you think I am a con man?"[6]

Coppola's varying views on Tucker did not, however, prove to be the source of the next screenplay by him that reached the screen. The next film to appear featuring his work was *The Great Gatsby*.

The Great Gatsby Script

This particular remake of *The Great Gatsby* was originally sched-uled for a 1971 production date. But the script turned in by Truman Capote was judged inadequate. Coppola entered the operation in the following year. As Jack Clayton, the director of *The Great Gatsby*, explained later, "Francis came in and did an absolute mira-cle job in time and speed in order to get us off . . . . But he could not stay on the script very long simply because he was just about to do another film."

Clayton also stated that only a few changes were made in the script Coppola wrote. "I think certain things from the book went back [into the script], certain lines were changed, but anything that was changed was *always* in the book."[7]

Coppola stated otherwise.

The difference of opinion is of some importance, for the film was severely criticized by the reviewers, and rightly so.

Fairly faithful to Fitzgerald's plot, the action in the film version is seen mainly through the eyes of Nick Carraway. Living on Long Island during the Prohibition Era, Carraway becomes friendly with Tom Buchanan, his wife Daisy, and another socialite, Jordan Baker. Carraway also attends some of the lavish parties given by Jay Gatsby and becomes acquainted with him, too.

Gradually Carraway learns certain facts. He learns that Tom and Daisy are unhappily married. He learns that Tom has a mistress named Myrtle, the wife of a gas-station owner, George Wilson. He learns that Gatsby and Daisy were once in love, but that, at the time, Gatsby had no money and, so, Daisy broke off their relationship.

Carraway agrees to Gatsby's plan: he invites Daisy and Gatsby to his home on the same day. The two former lovers meet, and Gatsby feels certain that Daisy is still as much in love with him as he is with her. In order to impress her with the wealth he has accumulated, he takes her to his palatial mansion.

Later, on a hot summer day, all the main characters meet and decide to drive to Manhattan. Tom Buchanan drives Gatsby's yellow car and stops at Wilson's gas station. In the city, Tom, Daisy, and Gatsby quarrel. Tom is particularly cutting, while Gatsby tries to hold back in order to spare Daisy's feelings. Daisy at times seems to side with Gatsby; at other times, she sides with her husband.

Because the outing has proven such a failure, they all decide to drive back to Long Island. Gatsby and Daisy are now in his car; Daisy, though upset, does the driving. When they pass Wilson's gas station, Myrtle—thinking Tom is still in the car—runs toward it. The distraught Daisy accidentally kills Myrtle and does not stop the car. Grief-stricken and bewildered, Wilson comes to think that Gatsby is responsible for the death of Myrtle. He hunts Gatsby down. Gatsby, confused and depressed concerning the situation between Daisy and himself, floats on a rubber raft in the middle of his pool. Wilson sneaks up to the side of the pool and shoots Gatsby dead.

Gatsby's father arrives in order to attend his son's funeral. But neither Daisy nor any of the other high society "friends" that Gatsby made appear at the service. The only other person there is Carraway.

Once again, it is hard to evaluate the screenplay that Coppola wrote because, although no one else is mentioned as being in any way responsible for the script, director Clayton did state that he changed "certain things." The problem, a typical one, centers on the question of what in the released version of the film was Coppola responsible for and what was Clayton (or somebody else) responsible for.

Certainly the pace of the picture, which was slow and tedious, would most likely be the fault of the director. So, too, Clayton, not Coppola, is to blame for the over-insistent photography and, to some extent, the poor acting. Then there is the matter of the interpretation of the characters. In the novel, Gatsby is shown to be very shrewd and quick-thinking when it comes to making money. But he is hopelessly blinded by love when it comes to anything concerning Daisy. He is too fascinated by his image of Daisy to realize that it was not really *just* his lack of wealth that caused her to reject him years ago. But in the movie, either because of what Coppola wrote or because of Clayton's or Robert Redford's interpretation, Gatsby's ignorance with regard to Daisy is softened into innocence.

Because of *somebody*, Mia Farrow's Daisy is a disaster. Farrow plays Daisy as a Tragic Young Thing—sweet, bewildered, caught, and blameless. It is principally because of this misinterpretation that *The Great Gatsby* is a dismal failure. The whole point of Fitzgerald's novel is that Jay Gatsby wastes his potentially fine character pursuing a self-indulgent, self-pitying, heartless young woman who enjoys nurturing romantic feelings in others and in herself as long as it costs her nothing to do so; for she will never forsake her upper-class cocoon.

Because the essential nature of Daisy is nowhere present in the film, the final meaning of this superb novel is totally lost. What Fitzgerald was ultimately alluding to was perhaps the most popular of all the Great American Myths: namely, that if you gain economic wealth, you will also gain Happiness. What Fitzgerald's story brilliantly dramatizes is that the American Myth is a resounding illusion. Gatsby is positive that if he is able to accumulate enough money, he will gain Happiness—Daisy. Then he gains fabulous wealth, but it does not bring him Daisy—Happiness. He has wasted his life pursuing an illusion.

None of this is dramatized in the version of *The Great Gatsby* for which Coppola wrote the script and which Clayton directed.

The movie was greeted with much harsh criticism. Yet Coppola, though given sole screen credit for the script, was treated rather kindly. Jay Cook, for instance, cited Coppola as scriptwriter, but quickly pointed out that the script was "much rejuggled by Director Clayton."[8]

Spurred by the film's reception, Coppola declared, "I don't enjoy the directing process. *Gatsby*'s a good point because if you had asked me the question whether I was a writer or a director before *Gatsby,* I would have said I was a writer and I just direct sometimes. But I was so impressed with how badly *Gatsby* worked that I started to put more credit to what a director does. He changed that script all around, and that's one thing. Aside from that, there were scenes in there that, in my opinion, had the wrong objectives and they were, in my opinion, ruined."

Coppola then cited one such scene, the scene featuring Gatsby's father at the end of the film. "It doesn't work at all in the movie. You ask yourself why the scene that sticks with you the most, and seems so touching and relevant in the book, seems like an unnecessary appendix on the movie. It has to do with the fact that when Nick opens the door and there's this old man standing there—in the movie, this old man is crying—he says, 'I've come from so-and-so to the funeral of my son.' It's already ruined at that point, because the whole intention was: this man thought his son had become a great man. He came in awe with an almost positive sense of what this boy did, what a fantastic life he led . . . . There was grief, of course, but the basic thrust was that the man was proud of his son."

Warming to his topic, Coppola said, "In *Gatsby,* I disagreed with the casting and I don't think the script ever got to see the light of day in the form that I think it should have . . . . [Clayton] changed the beginning, the middle, and the end . . . . My opening of *Gatsby* dealt with a number of details. My concept was, in a poetic way, to show you certain clues, through imagery: the yellow car in the garage, the house itself, Gatsby's room, his shirts, his clothes, pictures of Daisy, the newspaper clippings, and then the little Hopalong Cassidy book in which you actually see in a child's handwriting the little resolutions . . . . It was my premise that throughout the development of the film, each one of those little symbols would fit into place like parts of a puzzle."

Coppola discussed another main scene in the film. "The book of Gatsby has no real scene between Daisy and Gatsby . . . . Since the two stars would be Daisy and Gatsby, it was going to be obligatory to have a scene with them . . . . I came up with a concept that I liked a lot and I wrote it that way . . . . I wrote a scene between Daisy and Gatsby taking place in the bedroom with Gatsby sitting on a chair and Daisy sitting on the bed or something. They were far apart. It was my theory that they shouldn't even touch a lot or kiss or any of that stuff. I wrote a scene about seven or eight pages long of pure dialogue. A kind of acting tour de force between two actors in a room, nothing else . . . . Jack liked it very much but felt that it was too dry. He wanted to have scenes of the two of them walking through a field, or seeing birds, or lounging together. I was always against that. I felt that was like a Salem commercial."

Then Coppola described what actually evolved. Clayton "took that eight page scene and he chopped it into about five scenes . . . . He spread them throughout the last two-thirds of the movie, which is one of the reasons the movie became so interminable."

Clayton also changed the ending. "My ending had been dealing with finishing everything. The last scene was the scene of the father. The father comes in and you realize that the father's just this low-class guy. You really see Gatsby's roots by seeing who his father is. He says my name is Gatz. As he's up in his room packing his son's things, he takes out this book. He says, 'Look, this is a book he had when he was a kid. Even then he was going to make something out of himself.' He starts to read the little boyish dictates and it connects with the final image of the opening. When he finishes, he looks up and he sees the picture of Daisy, and he says, 'Who's this girl?' That was the end of the movie. So what I had set up at the beginning went all the way to the end."[9]

It would appear, then, that Coppola's script was much tighter and more dynamic than the final released version of the film. However, there is still not much evidence to indicate that Coppola had a decisively more perceptive understanding of the characters and theme than the interpretation presented on the screen under Clayton's direction.

But if Coppola's work on *The Great Gatsby* seemed unrewarding, Coppola was abundantly rewarded when the 1974 Academy Award winners were announced. Robert DeNiro, another actor whom Coppola helped to make a star, won an Oscar for his contribution to *The Godfather, Part II*. Because of their work in the same picture, Coppola's father, Carmine, shared with Fellini's long-time collaborator, Nino Rota, an Oscar for the best "original dramatic score," and Coppola's sister, Talia Shire, received a nomination as best supporting actress. More than that, the film was voted the best picture of the year. And Coppola, one of the film's producers, gained additional honors for having both directed it and co-authored the screenplay.

Apocalypse Now

By 1976, Coppola had assumed command of another major project, the making of *Apocalypse Now*. John Milius had written the first version of the script years earlier. The story is a variation of Joseph Conrad's *Heart of Darkness* and takes place during the Vietnam War. The basic plot of *Apocalypse Now* centers on an American officer who is told to sail up a Vietnam river and liquidate a group of Americans in the jungle who are shooting at American planes.

The original plan was for George Lucas to direct the film in a documentary style. As time went on, however, Coppola became more and more involved in the undertaking. He wanted the film to be the foundation on which his Coppola Company would build. He invested approximately one million dollars of his own money in the venture.

Coppola decided to film the story in the Philippines. This decision led some of the actors Coppola wanted in his film to back off from the project. The cast that was finally assembled featured Marlon Brando, Robert Duvall, and Martin Sheen. The production, now bankrolled by United Artists, was halted first when Brando left to spend an agreed-upon amount of time with his offspring. The second major halt occurred when a typhoon destroyed the sets.

Production costs edged toward thirty million dollars—which was ten million more than the allotted budget. Still, the schedule called for the film to be released in 1977. Once again, Coppola is risking a great amount of his money and his time—to say nothing of his reputation—on one film production.

Summary

Coppola does not wish to be judged as a writer-director in any final sense at this stage in his career. His wish is a valid one. It is one thing to offer broadly inclusive "final judgments" on the creative efforts of such directors as John Ford, Raoul Walsh, and Howard Hawks, all of whom have directed many decades' worth of films. At present, Coppola is not yet forty years old. It would be silly to try to "set" Coppola, to force him into some kind of pigeonhole.

Coppola has stated more than once that he has not yet attempted a truly major film—a film in which he utilizes all his craft and directs a script—written by himself—containing his fundamental insights and beliefs concerning the human experience. He considers that, despite whatever degree of success he has had, his films so far are all part of an ongoing apprenticeship.

But it is also true that every serious artist *always* feels that he is still going through an apprenticeship, still learning his craft. It is also true that while Coppola is not yet forty years old, he has been directing films for a good number of years, and writing films for almost as long a time.

It is not, then, unfair to use evaluations of the individual films Coppola has written and directed as a means of discussing his career as a whole up to the present time.

The first of the seven films he has directed, *Dementia 13*, is not a horror-film classic nor an embarrassment. It has some thoroughly effective sequences, and it has some bland or belabored scenes. Basically, the photography is adequate; the acting, pedestrian; and the dialogue, functional. The film is only of any special interest because it is the first full-length film that Coppola directed.

With regard to what have been called his "personal" films, *You're A Big Boy Now*, *The Rain People*, and *The Conversation*, the first is by far the best. The pace of both *The Rain People* and *The Conversation* is too slow. The stylistic shuttlings in *The Conversation* are a mistake. *The Rain People* is done in only one style, a semidocumentary style (aided by flashbacks), but it does not help the film very much. The plots of both pictures are weak. The main characters in *The Rain People* are exceptionally interesting, but they are not fully developed. In *The Conversation*, the main character, though interesting in the early scenes, is delineated even less successfully.

You're A Big Boy Now, all in all, holds up well. Coppola was no more technically innovative in this film than he was in his other two personal films. But the influence (stronger perhaps than Coppola has acknowledged) of Richard Lester and others was salutary. It encouraged Coppola to employ a fast pace, which fit the material perfectly. There was enough looseness in the script to allow Coppola to incorporate "bits of business" (especially in the chase scenes) that emerged during the on-location filming. Yet, as was not the case with his other two personal films, Coppola finished the screenplay for this film before the shooting began; and this might well account, in part, for the superior quality of *You're A Big Boy Now*. It includes an almost endless stream of clever "touches,"

touches that create very interesting nuances in characters that at first appear to be strictly stereotypes.

Of the bigger productions that Coppola directed, *Finian's Rainbow* is a failure. Most of the music holds up nicely, but it already had for a good number of years before the movie was made. The film contains a few successful comic moments, thanks mainly to Al Freeman, Jr. and Keenan Wynn. Petula Clark is pleasant to look at and listen to. That, however, is about it. The plot is woeful. The acting, according to Coppola himself, is quite poor. Fred Astaire is wasted. The photography is numbingly insistent on showing us people in motion.

But the two *Godfather* films are decisive successes. As a profound metaphorical study of the United States or a keen realistic study of the Mafia, the first *Godfather* fails. Nonetheless, it builds on the material in the novel with extraordinary skill. The long opening sequence, the wedding reception, holds our attention completely. And from the time Michael becomes centrally involved in the family's affairs (after his father is shot and hospitalized) to the last scene, the film is almost continuously riveting. It is an outstanding gangster film.

Coppola stated that *The Godfather, Part II* should really be categorized as one of his personal films. In some respects, he is right. He was almost completely responsible for the script. He was from the very start unquestionably in charge of filming the sequel. In other ways, however, *The Godfather, Part II* cannot be labeled one of his personal films. The picture was a munificently budgeted major studio production; and this circumstance bred an increasing number of intense pressures over which Coppola had no control. These pressures harassed Coppola into making many quick decisions with which he was not at all happy.

In any case, despite its flaws, the film graphically presents the descent into hell—or at least into hollowness—of its main contemporary character, Michael. It dramatizes the early life of Michael's father, Vito Corleone, a time in which Vito leads his family to prosperity. But it also implies that the climb to prosperity created problems that Michael, when he becomes the head of the family, copes with successfully in terms of wealth and power, but unsuccessfully in terms of the unity and happiness of the Corleone family. We see, finally, the disintegration of the family. Michael at the end is all-powerful, and all alone.

Except for *The Godfather, Part II*, none of Coppola's work would encourage one to predict that Coppola will someday be seriously compared with such filmmakers as Ingmar Bergman or Federico Fellini. His efforts at scripting *This Property Is Condemned, Is Paris Burning?*, and *The Great Gatsby* have added nothing to his stature as an artist. Nor did his work as director of *Dementia 13* and *Finian's Rainbow*. He has not yet directed a string of films that match the quality of work done by directors who are close to being his contemporaries—John Schlesinger, Lindsay Anderson, and François Truffaut. He has not been a successful innovator in the technical spheres of sound and photography. The "sound effects" in *The Conversation* were a failure. The camera work in his films has never broken new ground or extended the experiments of other filmmakers in any substantial and exciting way.

On the other hand, this still-young artist's work compares quite favorably with the work produced by Mike Nichols, Arthur Penn, Sam Peckinpah, Peter Bogdanovich, Haskell Wexler, Martin Scorsese, and many others. There is a maturity of attitude governing the violence in the second *Godfather* film in particular that is depressingly absent in *Bonnie and Clyde*, *Bullit*, and the films made by Sam Peckinpah and Martin Scorsese. For all its faults, *The Conversation* probes the contemporary scene in a deeper way than *Joe* or *Medium Cool* do. *The Rain People*, though not a success, is a far more honest "road picture" than *Easy Rider* and almost every other film of that genre. While full of fun, *You're A Big Boy Now* has a poignant, serious point that raises it above the slicker comedies of Mike Nichols and Peter Bogdanovich.

In fact, if Coppola's films are looked at carefully, Gerald Mast's statement that *The Conversation* is the first film by Coppola to reveal his "social conscience" becomes a highly questionable assessment. Coppola's moral awareness is clearly present in many of his films, beginning with *You're A Big Boy Now*. There are rich moral-social overtones in *The Rain People*. Coppola's musings about responsibility and about particular problems confronting the American woman (problems the women's liberation movement later focused on) serve as the foundation for this film. Then one comes to *The Conversation*, in which Coppola's valid moral observations are blunted by the flaws in the film. In *The Godfather, Part II*, however, the moral dimension blends beautifully with the other major elements in the movie. Though faulty and muddled at times, the moral outlook Coppola has brought to most of his films is one of the things that set him apart from many of his Hollywood contemporaries.

Another reason that Coppola deserves to be singled out for special credit concerns his adventurous probings of the possibility of emphasizing character more than plot in a medium that very much lends itself to enhancing plot more than character. Films thrive on completely stereotyped characters because such characters need no "explaining"—hence, do not cause any "delay" in the presentation of plenty of plot. So, too, the writer-director is pressured to present only that kind of stereotyped character—the cowboy, the detective, the racing car driver—who is frequently in motion.

Coppola, at his best, is an exceptionally fine creator of film characters. A host of only semi-stereotyped memorable characters appear in *You're A Big Boy Now*. All the main characters, and just about all of the minor ones, in *The Rain People* are unique and thoroughly interesting. Although Harry Caul in *The Conversation* proved too uptight, too elusive to allow Coppola to make him into a successful character delineation, Caul is still original and worth pondering. Coppola's portrait of General Patton is excellent. It also offers, in Patton's opening monologue, Coppola's successful attempt to present a character in an innovative way. In the two *Godfather* films, numerous characters break through the mere stereotypic. James Cagney could keep playing (marvelously) one basic gangster character in script after script. But Vito Corleone and Michael Corleone and Hyman Roth are by no means carbon copies of other gangster-film characters. They are all vividly individualistic.

This, in turn, partly explains why so many performers have greatly profited from appearing in films that Coppola has directed. The rest of the explanation is twofold. Coppola has an exceptionally keen eye for spotting potential talent. And he can sensitively direct this talent into producing top-quality performances in front of the camera. He is surely to be given much credit for aiding the careers of James Caan, Karen Black, Robert Duvall, Al Pacino, Diane Keaton, and Robert DeNiro. He gave Elizabeth Hartman the most interesting part she has had thus far in her career. And he gave showcase roles to Julie Harris, Rip Torn, Geraldine Page, Marlon Brando, Shirley Knight, John Cazale, and many others.

Coppola once commented, "There is no intermediate in this business. They either say, 'Here he is, the boy wonder, the best young filmmaker...' or they say. 'Ah, he's just a load of crap.' Why doesn't someone ever say, 'Well, he's a promising guy and he's somewhat intelligent and he's really trying and maybe in ten years he might be a really....' No one ever says that."[10] It is a good comment to keep in mind; for it is true that people connected with the motion picture industry tend to exaggerate.

Coppola's work at this point in his career does not put him in either extreme category. He has been slow in bringing a steadily mature vision to his film efforts. It is, in fact, still too early to tell whether he has yet achieved such a vision. He has also depended too much on his ability to improvise and to ad-lib while making a movie; what evidence we have indicates that he does a better job when at least a great deal of the work is carefully thought out before he steps onto the set.

But, as a director, he is an exceptionally knowledgeable craftsman. As a writer, he has adapted and co-authored several fine screenplays. In *The Godfather, Part II* he did his best job thus far in presenting a vivid, meaningful story and many gripping, rich characterizations in one film. And, because that film is such a recent effort, it is certainly not foolish to hope for more such high-quality work from him.

Notes and References

Chapter One

1. William Murray, "Playboy Interview: Francis Ford Coppola," *Playboy*, 22 (July, 1975), 185.

2. Susan Braudy, "Francis Ford Coppola: A Profile," *Atlantic Monthly*, 238 (August, 1976), 66.

3. Ibid., 69.

4. Maureen Orth, "Godfather of the Movies," *Newsweek*, November 24, 1974, p. 76.

5. Ibid.

6. Joseph Gelmis, "Francis Ford Coppola," in *The Film Director As Superstar* (Garden City, New York: Doubleday, 1970), p. 179.

7. Ibid.

8. Francis Ford Coppola, "The Garden of the Little Pink Princess," *The Word*, December, 1956, p. 15.

9. Murray, pp. 184–85.

10. "Alumnus Coppola Still Sparks Creative Fires," *The Hofstra Report*, 1 (October, 1975), 2–3.

11. Gelmis, p. 179.

12. Ibid.

13. Murray, p. 184.

14. Stephen Farber, "Coppola And *The Godfather*," *Sight And Sound*, 41 (Autumn, 1972), 219.

15. "Francis Ford Coppola on the Director," *Movie People*, ed. Fred Baker (New York: Lancer Books, 1973), p. 66.

16. Ibid.

17. Marjorie Rosen, "Francis Ford Coppola," *Film Comment*, 10 (July–August, 1974), 44–45.

18. "Francis Ford Coppola on the Director," p. 67.

19. Farber, p. 219.

20. Bill Davidson, "King of Schlock," *New York Times Magazine*, December 28, 1975, p. 30.

21. Ibid., p. 31.

22. Murray, p. 68.

23. "Francis Ford Coppola on the Director," p. 67.

24. Farber, p. 219.

25. "Francis Ford Coppola on the Director," pp. 68–69.

26. Farber, p. 219.

27. "Francis Ford Coppola on the Director," p. 69.

28. Ibid., p. 71.

29. Ibid., p. 70.

30. Axel Madsen, "Bogdanovich and Coppola," in *The New Hollywood* (New York: Thomas Y. Crowell, 1975), p. 110.

31. Gelmis, p. 180.

32. "Francis Ford Coppola on the Director," p. 84.

33. Farber, p. 220.

34. Gelmis, p. 180.

35. Howard Thompson, review of *Dementia 13*, as quoted in *Filmfacts*, 6 (November 7, 1963), 240.

36. Joseph Morgenstern, "A National Anthem," *Newsweek*, February 20, 1967, pp. 96, 98.

37. "Francis Ford Coppola," *Current Biography Yearbook 1974*, ed. Charles Moritz (New York: H. W. Wilson Company, 1975), p. 90.

38. Gelmis, p. 186.

39. "Francis Ford Coppola on the Director," pp. 85–86.

40. Ibid., p. 82.

41. Ibid., p. 71.

42. Gelmis, p. 181.

43. Bosley Crowther, review of *This Property Is Condemned*, *New York Times*, August 4, 1966, p. 24.

44. "Belle Wringer," *Time*, July 22, 1966, p. 62.

45. Hollis Alpert, "Instant Tennessee Williams," *Saturday Review*, June 25, 1966, p. 40.

46. "Francis Ford Coppola on the Director," pp. 72–74. (Extracts used in the three paragraphs preceding reference 46 are from this source.)

47. Gelmis, p. 181.

48. "Francis Ford Coppola on the Director," p. 73.

49. Madsen, pp. 110–11.

50. Brendon Gill, "Gone Wrong," *New Yorker*, November 19, 1966, p. 183.

51. Joseph Morgenstern, "City of Dullness," *Newsweek*, November 21, 1966, p. 126.

52. Bosley Crowther, review of *Is Paris Burning?*, *New York Times*, November 11, 1966, p. 36.

53. "Bang-I-Gotcha!" *Time*, November 25, 1966, as quoted in *Filmfacts*, 9 (December 1, 1966), p. 264.

Chapter Two

1. "Francis Ford Coppola on the Director," pp. 74–75.
2. Gelmis, pp. 182–83.
3. "Francis Ford Coppola on the Director," pp. 75–76.
4. Ibid., pp. 76–77.
5. Ibid., pp. 77–78.
6. Farber, p. 220.
7. "Francis Ford Coppola on the Director," pp. 79–80.
8. Morgenstern, "A National Anthem," p. 96. Howard Thompson, review of *You're A Big Boy Now, New York Times*, March 21, 1967, p. 35.
9. Gelmis, p. 182.

Chapter Three

1. Farber, p. 220.
2. Ibid.
3. Gelmis, p. 183.
4. Ibid., pp. 183, 185.
5. Ibid., pp. 184–85.
6. Murray, p. 65.
7. Gelmis, pp. 184–86.
8. Farber, p. 220.
9. Ibid.
10. Gelmis, p. 183.

Chapter Four

1. Farber, p. 220.
2. Gelmis, p. 187.
3. Farber, pp. 221–22.

Chapter Five

1. Gelmis, pp. 187–90.
2. "Francis Ford Coppola on the Director," p. 87.
3. Farber, p. 222.
4. Madsen, pp. 113–14.
5. Farber, p. 222.
6. Madsen, p. 111.
7. Farber, p. 220.
8. Ibid.
9. Stanley Kauffmann, *Figures Of Light* (New York: Harper & Row, 1971), p. 236.
10. Rex Reed, *Big Screen, Little Screen* (New York: Macmillan, 1971), p. 272.

11. Vincent Canby, review of *Patton*, *New York Times*, February 5, 1970, p. 33.

12. Joseph Morgenstern, "Magnificent Anachronism," *Newsweek*, February 16, 1970, pp. 91–92.

Chapter Six

1. Mario Puzo, "The Making of 'The Godfather,' " in *The Godfather Papers* (Greenwich, Conn. Fawcett Crest, 1973), pp. 34–36, 38, 42–43, 58–59.

2. Murray, p. 56.

3. Ibid.

4. Joseph Gelmis, "How Brando Brought Don Corleone to Life," *Films 72–73*, ed. David Denby (Indianapolis: Bobbs-Merrill, 1973), p. 12.

5. Ibid.

6. Murray, pp. 56, 58.

7. Puzo, pp. 60–63.

8. Bob Thomas, *Marlon* (New York: Random House, 1973), pp. 236–37.

9. Farber, p. 222.

10. Murray, p. 58.

11. Farber, p. 222.

12. Ibid., p. 223.

13. Rena Andrews, "Francis Ford Coppola—On Top of the Film World and Still Rising," *Biography News*, 2 (January/February, 1975), 48.

14. Murray, p. 58.

15. Ibid., p. 65.

16. Farber, pp. 222–23.

Chapter Seven

1. Mario Puzo, *The Godfather* (Greenwich, Conn.: Fawcett Crest, 1969), pp. 325–27.

2. Murray, p. 60.

3. William S. Pechter, "Keeping Up with the Corleones," *Films 72–73*, ed. David Denby (Indianapolis: Bobbs-Merrill, 1973), pp. 6–7.

4. Gay Talese, *Honor Thy Father* (New York: World Publishing, 1971), p. 76.

5. Murray, p. 62.

6. Talese, p. 308.

7. Andrew Sarris, as quoted in *Filmfacts*, ed. Ernest Parmentier, 15, No. 4 (1972), 71.

8. Farber, p. 223.

9. Paul D. Zimmerman, " 'The Godfather': Triumph for Brando," *Newsweek*, March 13, 1972, p. 57.

10. Farber, p. 223.

11. Luigi Barzini, *The Italians* (New York: Bantam, 1965), p. 284.

12. Pauline Kael, "Alchemy," *Deeper Into Movies* (Boston: Atlantic–Little, Brown, 1973), p. 420.

13. Ibid.

14. Gary Arnold, review of *The Godfather*, as quoted in *Filmfacts*, ed. Ernest Parmentier, 15, iv (1972), 74.

15. Stanley J. Solomon, *Beyond Formula* (New York: Harcourt Brace Jovanovich, 1976), pp. 167, 194.

16. Murray, p. 65.

17. Thomas, p. 247.

18. Stanley Kauffmann, *Living Images* (New York: Harper & Row, 1975), p. 104.

19. Farber, p. 219.

20. Murray, p. 60.

Chapter Eight

1. Farber, p. 223.

2. John Rockwell, " 'My Own Little City, My Own Little Opera...' " *Saturday Review*, 55 (December 2, 1972), 57–58.

3. Susan Braudy, "Ah, Coppola," *Atlantic Monthly*, 238 (October, 1976), 34.

4. Paul Gardner, "Alumni of Film School Now 'Star' as Directors," *New York Times*, January 30, 1974, p. 24.

5. Rosen, pp. 43–44, 48–49.

6. Orth, p. 80.

7. Kauffmann, *Living Images*, pp. 276–77.

8. Gerald Mast, *A Short History of the Movies* (Indianapolis: Bobbs-Merrill, 1976), p. 489.

9. David Denby, "Stolen Privacy," *Sight And Sound*, 43 (Summer, 1974), 132.

10. Rosen, p. 44.

11. William S. Pechter, "Coppola's Progress," *Commentary*, 58 (July, 1974), 63.

12. Rosen, p. 44.

Chapter Nine

1. Murray, p. 58.

2. Rosen, p. 45.

3. Murray, p. 60.

4. Orth, p. 75.

5. Rosen, p. 48.

6. Murray, pp. 62, 65.

7. Orth, p. 74.

8. Murray, pp. 60, 62.

9. "The Final Act of a Family Epic," *Time*, December 16, 1974, pp. 73–74.

10. Stanley Kauffmann, review of *The Godfather, Part II*, *New Republic*, January 18, 1975, p. 22.

11. Pauline Kael, "Fathers And Sons," *New Yorker*, December 23, 1974, p. 65.

12. Orth, p. 74.

13. John Yates, "Godfather Saga: The Death of the Family," *Journal of Popular Film*, 4, ii (1975), 162.

Chapter Ten

1. Katrine Ames (with William J. Cook), "Godfather III," *Newsweek*, July 21, 1975, p. 34.

2. Elizabeth Peer (with William J. Cook), "City Slickers," *Newsweek*, September 1, 1975, p. 42.

3. Murray, p. 184.

4. Orth, p. 80.

5. Murray, p. 68.

6. Braudy, "Francis Ford Coppola: A Profile," p. 73.

7. Rosen, p. 49.

8. Jay Cook, "The Crack-Up," *Time*, April 1, 1974, p. 88.

9. Rosen, pp. 46–47.

10. Gelmis, p. 187.

Selected Bibliography

1. Books

PUZO, MARIO. *The Godfather*. Greenwich, Conn. Fawcett Crest, 1969. The novel is of obvious value to anyone interested in Coppola's two most famous films. Reading this book can lead one to realize how succinct, *not* long and rambling, the film version of *The Godfather* is.

TALESE, GAY. *Honor Thy Father*. New York: World Publishing, 1971. Although this study of Bill Bonanno, a high-ranking member of the Mafia, is only intermittently interesting, it does offer the reader who has seen *The Godfather* films an opportunity to compare the domestic world of the Bonannos with that of the Corleones.

2. Sections from Books

BAKER, FRED, editor. "Francis Ford Coppola on the Director" in *Movie People*, pp. 66–88. New York: Lancer Books, 1973. This early interview focuses on Coppola's career through the completion of *You're A Big Boy Now* and provides valuable detailed information concerning Coppola's work for Roger Corman (including the *Dementia 13* project) and the filming of *You're A Big Boy Now*.

GELMIS, JOSEPH. "Francis Ford Coppola" in *The Film Director As Superstar*, pp. 177–90. Garden City, New York: Doubleday, 1970. Covering Coppola's career up to the completion of *The Rain People*, this interview concentrates at length on Coppola's stint as a Seven Arts screenwriter and on the making of *Dementia 13*, *You're A Big Boy Now*, and *Finian's Rainbow*. The interview, which took place just as *Finian's Rainbow* was released, also dramatically reveals a tense, tired Coppola given to emotional outbursts.

_____. "How Brando Brought Don Corleone to Life" in *Films 72–73*, pp. 11–15. Edited by David Denby. Indianapolis: Bobbs-Merrill, 1973. A concise report on how Brando became a cast member of *The Godfather* and then set standards the other actors sought to match.

KAEL, PAULINE. "Alchemy" in *Deeper Into Movies*, pp. 420–26. Boston: Atlantic–Little, Brown, 1973. An extremely thorough analysis of *The Godfather*, Kael's review also suggests that, in metaphorical terms, the

187

188

film can be seen as "our nightmare" of "what we fear Americanism to be."

KAUFFMANN, STANLEY. Reviews of *The Godfather* and *The Conversation* in *Living Images*, pp. 104–105, 276–77. New York: Harper & Row, 1975. The book contains two short pieces of special interest: a review of *The Godfather* that details why Kauffmann considers Brando's performance a poor one; and a review of *The Conversation* analyzing Harry Caul and praising Coppola for his attempt to assimilate European cinematic techniques.

MADSEN, AXEL. "Bogdanovich and Coppola" in *The New Hollywood*, pp. 108–16. New York: Thomas Y. Crowell, 1975. A breezy account of Coppola's career, this recapitulation reprints some interesting quotes from previous material, but offers almost nothing in the way of analysis or insight.

MAST, GERALD. "The New American *Auteurs*" in *A Short History Of The Movies*. Second Edition, pp. 489–90. Indianapolis: Bobbs-Merrill, 1976. Summarizes Coppola's career in a long paragraph that emphasizes the two distinct types of films—the "commercial projects" and the "personal" projects—Coppola has made, and, then, succinctly states a very affirmative view of *The Conversation*.

PECHTER, WILLIAM S. "Keeping Up with the Corleones" in *Films 72–73*, pp. 4–9. Edited by David Denby. Indianapolis: Bobbs-Merrill, 1973. Centering on the significance of *The Godfather* in relation to the genre of the gangster movie, this essay suggests that Coppola's film both operates within and alters that genre.

PUZO, MARIO. "The Making of 'The Godfather' " in *The Godfather Papers*, pp. 32–69. Greenwich, Conn.: Fawcett Crest, 1973. A rambling, conversationally-casual, but entertaining "history" of how Puzo came to write his best seller and of Puzo's part in the filming of his book. Indirectly, one learns how minor a role the writer plays in a Hollywood production.

SOLOMON, STANLEY J. *"The Godfather* (1972)" in *Beyond Formula*, pp. 194–98. New York: Harcourt Brace Jovanovich, 1976. Perhaps the most insightful of all the commentaries on *The Godfather*, this analysis also presents the best case offered by those who believe the Mafia-United States metaphor is a valid one.

3. Periodicals

ANON. "The Final Act of a Family Epic." *Time*, December 16, 1974, pp. 70–74. A gossipy, therefore entertaining, report of the behind-the-scenes activity during the filming of *The Godfather, Part II*.

ARNOLD, GARY. Review of *The Godfather*, as quoted in *Filmfacts*, ed. Ernest Parmentier, 15, iv (1972): 73–74. What is of special value in this review is the author's perceptive analysis of Coppola's creative efforts as a writer as well as director through the completion of *The God-father*.

BRAUDY, SUSAN. "Ah, Coppola." *Atlantic Monthly*, 238 (October 1976): 34. Here, in her response to a letter of inquiry, the author succinctly summarizes Coppola's significant contribution to the making of *American Graffiti*.

———. "Francis Ford Coppola: A Profile." *Atlantic Monthly*, 238 (August 1976): 66–73. In addition to the perfunctory recapitulation of Coppola's career up to the time of writing, the article is of particular interest because of its descriptions of Coppola at work in his San Francisco office and of Coppola's routine on location while filming *Apocalypse Now*.

DENBY, DAVID. "Stolen Privacy." *Sight And Sound*, 43 (Summer 1974): 131–33. A long, perceptive analysis of *The Conversation* which does not ignore flaws in the film, but which stresses its positive features. The author sums up the film as "a Hitchcockian thriller, a first-rate psychological portrait," and an "attack on American business values."

FARBER, STEPHEN. "Coppola And *The Godfather*." *Sight And Sound*, 41 (Autumn 1972): 217–23. This article contains three segments: a brief recapitulation of Coppola's early career; a detailed analysis of *The Godfather* which cites the Don as "a perfect example of the American self-made man"; and, the best segment, an interview in which Coppola comments at length about many stages of his career, particularly about the making of *The Rain People* and *The Godfather*.

KAEL, PAULINE. "Fathers And Sons." *New Yorker*, December 23, 1974, pp. 63–66. As thorough as her review of the first *Godfather* film, this writer's analysis of Michael and of how Coppola's sequel used and added to the thematic motifs in its predecessor is particularly acute.

KAUFFMANN, STANLEY. Review of *The Godfather, Part II*. *New Republic*, January 18, 1975, p. 22. Perhaps the best adverse criticism of a film which most critics applauded.

MORGENSTERN, JOSEPH. "A National Anthem." *Newsweek*, February 20, 1967, pp. 96, 98. This article not only waxes more enthusiastic about *You're A Big Boy Now* than most of the initial criticism did, but it also contains one of the first interviews with Coppola, the one in which Coppola compares himself to Hitler.

———. "Magnificent Anachronism." *Newsweek*, February 16, 1970, pp. 91–92. A review of *Patton* that presents a particularly strong case for judging the delineation of General Patton as ultimately "muddled."

MURRAY, WILLIAM. "Playboy Interview: Francis Ford Coppola." *Playboy*, 22 (July 1975): 53–54, 56, 58, 60, 62, 65, 68, 184–85. This long, in-depth interview, conducted after the release of *The Godfather, Part II*, has a wealth of information about the making of that film and its predecessor; it also contains Coppola's views on a wide range of general and personal matters.

ORTH, MAUREEN. "Godfather of the Movies." *Newsweek*, November 14, 1974, pp. 74–76, 80. A nicely-done résumé of Coppola's career and a close-up view of his life style after the success of *The Godfather*. It portrays Coppola at his most flamboyant.

PECHTER, WILLIAM S. "Coppola's Progress." *Commentary*, 58 (July 1974): 61–64. An astute scrutiny of *The Conversation* that praises its virtues, yet concentrates primarily on its flaws. The author compares the film to *Blow-Up* and discusses its relation to Coppola's other works, especially *The Rain People*.

ROCKWELL, JOHN. " 'My Own Little City, My Own Little Opera...' " *Saturday Review*, 55 (December 2, 1972): 56–58. An amusing, if somewhat patronizing report on Coppola's stint as director of a production of Gottfried von Einem's opera *The Visit of the Old Lady*.

ROSEN, MARJORIE. "Francis Ford Coppola." *Film Comment*, 10 (July–August, 1974): 43–49. Though loose in structure, this interview contains a fascinating sequence in which Coppola compares what he attempted to do in his script for *The Great Gatsby* with what the director Jack Clayton actually did during production. This interview is immediately followed by another with Clayton.

YATES, JOHN. "Godfather Saga: The Death of the Family." *Journal of Popular Film*, 4, ii (1975): 157–163. Although it starts off slowly, this essay is of value because it focuses on the *Godfather* films' Corleone family *not* as a metaphor for the United States, but as a family, especially as a family which finally "falls apart."

Filmography

DEMENTIA 13 (Filmgroup, Inc., 1963)
  (Title in Great Britain, THE HAUNTED AND THE HUNTED)
Producer: Roger Corman
Associate Producer: Marianne Wood
Assistant Director: Richard Dalton
Screenplay: Francis Coppola
Photography: Charles Hannawalt
Art Direction: Albert Locatelli
Set Decoration: Eleanor Neil
Music: Ronald Stein
Editor: Stewart O'Brien
Cast: William Campbell (Richard Haloran), Luana Anders (Louise Halo-
  ran), Bart Patton (Billy Haloran), Mary Mitchell (Kane), Patrick Magee
  (Justin Caleb), Peter Read (John Haloran)
Running Time: 81 minutes
Premiere: September 25, 1963, Los Angeles
16mm rental: United Films (Tulsa, Oklahoma), Westcoast Films (San Fran-
  cisco); sale, United Productions of America, 230 Park Avenue, New
  York, NY 10017

YOU'RE A BIG BOY NOW (Seven Arts, 1967)
Producer: Phil Feldman
Associate Producer: William Fadiman
Assistant Director: Larry Sturhahn
Screenplay: Francis Ford Coppola, based on the novel by David
  Benedictus
Photography: Andy Laszlo
Art Direction: Vassele Fotopoulos
Set Decoration: Marvin March
Music: Robert Prince
Musical Arranger and Conductor: Arthur Schroeck (Songs: "Darling, Be
  Home Soon," "You're A Big Boy Now," "Kite Chase," "Letter To Bar-
  bara," "Lonely (Amy's Theme)," "March," "Miss Thing's Thang," "Try

191

To Be Happy," and "Wash Her Away" by John Sebastian—sung by
The Lovin' Spoonful)
Sound: Jean Bagley, Sanford Rackow, Jack Jacobsen
Editor: Aram Avakian
Miss Hartman's Choreography: Robert Tucker
Costumes: Theoni V. Aldredge
Cast: Peter Kastner (Bernard Chanticleer), Elizabeth Hartman (Barbara
Darling), Geraldine Page (Margery Chanticleer), Julie Harris (Miss
Thing), Rip Torn (I. H. Chanticleer), Tony Bill (Raef), Karen Black
(Amy), Michael Dunn (Richard Mudd)
Running Time: 96 minutes
Premiere: December 9, 1966, Los Angeles (The film was premiered at this
time in order to qualify for the 1966 Academy Awards. It was not,
however, released nationally until 1967 and is usually dated 1967.)
16mm rental: MacMillan and many other national agencies.

FINIAN'S RAINBOW (Warner Brothers–Seven Arts, 1968)
Producer: Joseph Landon
Associate Producer: Joel Freeman
Assistant Directors: Fred Gammon, Howard Kazanjian
Screenplay: E. Y. Harburg, Fred Saidy
Photography: Philip Lathrop
Production Designer: Hilyard M. Brown
Set Decorations: William L. Kuehl
   (Sometimes Philip Abramson is also listed here)
Music: Burton Lane
Lyrics: E. Y. Harburg
Music: Supervised and Conducted by Ray Heindorf
Associate Music Supervisor: Ken Darby
Choreography: Hermes Pan
Musical numbers: "This Time of the Year" (Chorus); "How Are Things In
Glocca Morra?" (Sharon and Finian); "Look to the Rainbow" (Sharon,
Woody, and Finian); "If This Isn't Love" (Woody, Sharon, Finian, and
Chorus); "Something Sort Of Grandish" (Og and Sharon); "That Great
Come-And-Get-It Day" (Woody, Sharon, Chorus, and Ensemble);
"Old Devil Moon" (Woody and Sharon); "When the Idle Poor Become
the Idle Rich" (Finian, Sharon, and Chorus); "When I'm Not Near The
Girl I Love" (Og); "Rain Dance Ballet" (Susan and Chorus); "The
Begat" (Rawkins and the Passion Pilgrim Gospeleers)
   (Sometimes "Necessity" is also listed in the credits; but this number
   was deleted from the final print.)
Sound: M. A. Merrick, Dan Wallin
Editor: Melvin Shapiro
Costumes: Dorothy Jeakins

Cast: Fred Astaire (Finian McLonergan), Petula Clark (Sharon McLonergan), Tommy Steele (Og), Don Franks (Woody Mahoney), Keenan Wynn (Senator Rawkins), Al Freeman, Jr. (Howard), Barbara Hancock (Susan the Silent)
Running time: 145 minutes
Premiere: October 9, 1968, New York.
16mm rental: MacMillan and many other national distributors; lease: Warner Brothers Non-Theatrical Division, 4000 Warner Boulevard, Burbank, Cal. 91503

THE RAIN PEOPLE (Warner Brothers–Seven Arts, 1969)
Producers: Bart Patton, Ronald Colby
Production Associates: George Lucas, Mona Skager
Assistant Directors: Richard C. Bennett, Jack Cunningham
Screenplay: Francis Ford Coppola
Photography: Wilmer Butler
Art Direction: Leon Ericksen
Music: Ronald Stein
Music Associate: Carmen Coppola
Sound: Nathan Boxer, Walter Murch
Editor: Blackie Malkin
Cast: Shirley Knight (Natalie Ravenna), James Caan (Jimmie Kilgannon), Robert Duvall (Gordon), Tom Aldredge (Mr. Alfred)
Running Time: 102 minutes
Premiere: August 27, 1969, New York
16mm rental: Warner Brothers Non-Theatrical Division

THE GODFATHER (Paramount, 1972)
Producer: Albert S. Ruddy
Associate Producer: Gray Fredcrickson
Assistant Directors: Fred Gallo, Steve Skloot, Tony Brandt
Screenplay: Francis Ford Coppola and Mario Puzo, based on the novel by Mario Puzo.
Photography: Gordon Willis
Art Direction: Warren Clymer
Set Decoration: Philip Smith
Music: Nino Rota
Sound: Bud Grenzbach, Richard Portman, Christopher Newman, Les Lazarowitz
Editors: William Reynolds, Peter Zinner, Marc Laub, Murray Solomon
Costumes: Anna Hill Johnstone
Cast: Marlon Brando (Don Vito Corleone), Al Pacino (Michael Corleone), James Caan (Sonny Corleone), Richard Castellano (Clemenza), Robert Duvall (Tom Hagen), Diane Keaton (Kay Adams), Sterling Hayden (McCluskey), Talia Shire (Connie Rizzi), John Cazale (Fredo Corleone)

Running Time: 175 minutes
Premiere: March 11, 1972, New York. The date of the world premiere is not
    known.
16mm rental: Films, inc.

THE CONVERSATION (Paramount, 1974)
Producers: Francis Ford Coppola, Fred Roos
Screenplay: Francis Ford Coppola
Photography: Bill Butler
Production Design: Dean Tavoularis
Music: David Shire
Editors: Richard Chew, Walter Murch (who also worked on the sound
    track)
Cast: Gene Hackman (Harry Caul), John Cazale (Stan), Allen Garfield
    (Bernie Moran), Cindy Williams (Ann), Frederic Forrest (Mark)
Running time: 113 minutes
Premiere: April 7, 1974, New York. The date of the world premiere is not
    known.
16mm rental: Films, Inc.

THE GODFATHER, PART II (Paramount, 1974)
Producers: Francis Ford Coppola, Gray Frederickson, Fred Roos
Associate Producer: Mona Skager
Assistant Directors: Newton Arnold, Henry J. Lange, Jr., Chuck Myers,
    Alan Hopkins, Burt Bluestein, Tony Brandt
Screenplay: Francis Ford Coppola, Mario Puzo, based on the novel by
    Mario Puzo
Photography: Gordon Willis
Art Direction: Angelo Graham
Production Design: Dean Tavoularis
Set Decoration: George R. Nelson
Music: Nino Rota
Additional Music: Carmine Coppola
Editors: Peter Zinner, Barry Malkin, Richard Marks
Costumes: Theadora Van Runkle
Cast: Al Pacino (Michael), Robert Duvall (Tom Hagen), Diane Keaton
    (Kay), Robert DeNiro (Vito Corleone), John Cazale (Fredo Corleone),
    Talia Shire (Connie Corleone), Lee Strasberg (Hyman Roth), Michael
    V. Gazzo (Frankie Pentangeli)
Running Time: 200 minutes
Premiere: December 12, 1974, New York. The date of the world premiere
    is not known.
16mm rental: Films, Inc.

Index